Software for Pricing Options

SECOND EDITION

by Kenneth R. Trester

and Robert P. Swanson, Programmer

Institute For Options Research Inc.

LICENSE AGREEMENT

Opening the OPTION MASTER® software diskette package indicates your acceptance of the terms and conditions of this agreement, and your agreement to abide by them. You are granted a personal license to use the OPTION MASTER® software under the terms stated in this agreement. You may not assign or transfer the OPTION MASTER® software or this license to any other person without the express written consent of the Institute for Options Research, Inc. Any attempt to sub-license, assign or transfer any of the rights, duties or obligations hereunder is void. You may not copy, modify, alter, or electronically transfer or lease the software of this manual. The license is effective until termination. You may terminate it at any time by destroying the OPTION MASTER® software. It will also terminate if you fail to comply with any terms or conditions of this agreement.

LIMITED WARRANTY

The OPTION MASTER® software is provided "as is," without warranty of any kind, either expressed or implied, including, but not limited to, the limited warranties or merchantability and fitness for a particular purpose. The exclusion of implied warranties is not permitted by some states. The above exclusion may not apply to you. This warranty provides you with specific legal rights. There may be other rights that you may have which vary from state to state.

The entire risk as to the quality and performance of this program is with the purchaser. Should the program prove defective following your purchase, you, and not the manufacturer, distributor or retailer assumes the entire cost of all necessary servicing or repair.

Institute for Options Research, Inc. in no event will be liable to you for any damages, including any lost profit, lost sales, or any consequential damages arising out of the use or inability to use such software.

This disclaimer includes but is not limited to any interruption of service, loss of business, or anticipatory profits or losses or consequential damages resulting from the use or operation of such computer programs. However, Institute for Options Research, Inc. warrants the diskette on which the software is presented to be free from defects in materials and workmanship under normal use for 90 days from the date of purchase. Institute for Options Research, Inc.'s entire liability and your exclusive remedy shall be the replacement of any diskette not meeting the "limited warranty."

With regards to the Apple II version, Apple Computer, Inc. makes no warranties, either express or implied, regarding the enclosed computer software package, its merchantability or its fitness for any particular purpose. The exclusion of implied warranties is not permitted by some states. The above exclusion may not apply to you. This warranty provides you with specific legal rights. There may be other rights that you may have which vary from state to state.

DOS 3.3 is a copyrighted program of Apple Computer, Inc. licensed to Institute for Options Research, Inc. to distribute for use only in combination with OPTION MASTER®. Apple Software shall not be copied onto another diskette (except for archive purposes) or into memory unless as part of the execution of OPTION MASTER®. When OPTION MASTER® has completed execution, Apple Software shall not be used by any other program.

Publisher's Note: Although great care has been taken to present factual and accurate information, the Institute for Options Research, Inc. does not assume responsibility for the methodology or the accuracy of the material presented herein. Moreover, both publishers and authors will not be responsible for any resulting losses or profits in the past, present or future.

Users of the OPTION MASTER® software should recognize that all results generated by OPTION MASTER® are strictly theoretical, and should have no reflection on past, present or future option prices, and users should recognize that risk is involved in any option or security investment and you should not assume that any formula, method, chart, theory or philosophy can guarantee profitable results or equal past performances. This software should only be used by sophisticated investors who are fully aware of the risks in option trading. No solicitation to buy or sell securities or options is implied.

Printed in the USA.

CONTENTS

SECTION I: HOW TO USE OPTION MASTER

Chapter 1 - Introduction 3
OPTION MASTER®, Your Bluebook to the Options Markets 3
Options Defined 3
The Importance of Option Pricing 4
The Determinants of the Option Price 5
Where To Start 6
Chapter 2 - Getting Started 8
OPTION MASTER® for Windows™ 8
Software Requirements 8
Installation 8
Getting Started 9
Moving Around the Screen 10
Calculate 10
Prices 10
Probabilities 11
Ratios 12
Volatility 13
OPTION MASTER® for DOS 13
Installation 14
Getting Started 14
Moving Around the Screen 15
ALT Commands 16
Calculate 16
Prices 17
Probabilities 18
Ratios 18
Volatility 19
OPTION MASTER® on the Macintosh® 21
Installation 21
The Menu 21
Single Option Price 21
Multiple Option Prices 22
Calculate Volatility 22
Commodity Option Prices 23
Probability of Profit 23
OPTION MASTER® for Newton™ 24
Requirements 24
Installation 24
Getting Started 25
Calculate 26
Prices 26

Probabilities. . . . 27
Ratios 27
Volatility 28
Entry Tips 30
Chapter 3 - Using OPTION MASTER® 31
Quick and Easy 31
A Practice Session 31
Pricing Several Options 35
Calculating Futures Options Prices 37
Another Practice Session 38
Multiple Futures Options 39
Other Commodities 42
Chapter 4 - The Name of the Game is Volatility 44
Some Practice Sessions 46
Using Implied Volatility 49
A Practice Session 50
Chapter 5 - What Are Your Odds of Profiting? 53
Measuring Probability of Profit 53
Using the Probability of Profit Module 54
Chapter 6 - Behold the "Greeks" 59
Chapter 7 - Other Factors that Influence an Option's Price 61

SECTION II: HOW TO TRADE OPTIONS

Chapter 8 - The Secret to Success in the Options Game 65
The Forgotten Secret to Success 65
Unlocking the Secret 65
Why Options? 66
A Matter of Odds 67
The Secret – Scientifically Pricing Options 68
The Key to the Treasure Chest 69
The Art of Pricing Options 69
Chapter 9 - Playing the Index Options –
The Art of Pricing Index Options 73
The Hottest Game in Town 73
Option Buyers Beware 74
The Impact of Futures on Index Option Pricing 74
Active Traders Beware 76
Spreading – A Better Alternative 77
Chapter 10 - Buying Options for High and Consistent Profits 78
Plan Before You Play 78
The 10% Solution 79
Selecting the Best Option Buy Candidates 80
Options Before the Underlying Stock or Futures 80
The Best Priced Options 81
Super Cheap Options 81
Slightly In-The-Money Options 82
Secrets of the Professional Trader 83
When to Cut Losses 83
Let Your Profits Run 83
The "Round Robin" Approach 84

SECTION I

HOW TO USE OPTION MASTER®

CHAPTER 1 - INTRODUCTION

OPTION MASTER®: YOUR BLUEBOOK TO THE OPTIONS MARKETS

OPTION MASTER® is designed to help you determine whether a stock, index or futures option is fairly priced, and to determine whether an option is over- or underpriced. Similar to the purpose of the "blue book" that is utilized in the used car market, OPTION MASTER® is designed to tell you what the fair price of an option should be in a quick and easy manner.

OPTION MASTER® allows you to select the best option for a stock, commodity or index such as the S & P 100 Index, and does this by evaluating all of the options for that index, determining what their fair price should be. Unlike other option pricing programs, there is no need in this program for accessing an expensive data base, incurring high telephone charges, or buying additional hardware. Just a few easy entries into OPTION MASTER® will allow you to determine the fair price for a whole set of options. OPTION MASTER® is so easy to use that within a few minutes you can easily evaluate all the options for a whole series of stocks, indexes or commodities.

OPTIONS DEFINED

For option novices, much of the confusion regarding options can be removed if you look at listed options as side bets. Call options are side bets that the underlying common stock (index or futures) will rise in price above the strike price; put options are side bets that the underlying instrument will fall in price below the strike price.

These side bets have time limits of a few days to several years. The price you pay for this bet is determined on the option exchanges, and the price changes from moment to moment during the trading day. The price you pay for a put or a call is usually determined by the time left in the option (the expiration date), and how close the underlying stock price is to the strike price.

For example, a Ford Motors March 40 call is an option that expires on the third Friday in March. This option's strike price is 40. Each option is for 100 shares of stock, so if this option is priced at 1/2 (or .50), it is really priced at $50 (.50 X 100 = $50). Options that are not past the strike price are out-of-the-money.

The price you pay for out-of-the-money options is purely the anticipated value of the option. In other words, this price is an anticipation of the real in-the-money (or into the strike price) worth of the option at expiration. If the underlying stock price does not move through the strike price before the expiration date, the option will have no value.

For each point that the underlying stock price is in-the-money, the option is worth $100 more. For example, if Ford Motors is priced at 44, a Ford Motors 40 call in March before expiration would be worth at least $400. When there is little time left before an option expires, the anticipated value (or time value) of the option is quite small. Here, out-of-the-money puts and calls will have cheap price tags. In other words, you can make a small investment, with a chance to make a large profit.

THE IMPORTANCE OF OPTION PRICING

The most important key to success in the options market is not picking the right stock, but paying the right price for an option when you buy one, or when you write (sell) an option. Almost all market makers on the option exchanges and most option professionals are using option pricing models like OPTION MASTER® all the time to determine whether options are underpriced or overpriced according to such pricing models.

Now, with OPTION MASTER®, you have the same advantage that the professionals have. The pricing of options is so important because when you pay too much for an option – even if the underlying stock or commodity futures price on which that option is purchased moves in the right direction – you probably will not get enough reward for your potential risk. In a sense, you have stacked the odds against yourself. On the other side of the coin, when you buy underpriced options, you will get far more rewards compared to your risks when the underlying stock, index or commodity moves in the right direction. Now you have stacked the odds in your favor.

The goal of all option investors should always be to buy only options that are fairly priced – and better yet – underpriced according to a pricing model such as OPTION MASTER®. (Investors who write options should always attempt to write options that are overpriced, where they will receive more premium than the fair price of the option.)

Always remember: when you buy overpriced options, you stack the odds against you, but when you buy underpriced options, you stack the odds in your favor.

THE DETERMINANTS OF THE OPTION PRICE

There are several factors that determine what the option price will be and how the option price will change. These include the following:

1. The underlying stock, index or futures price.
2. The strike price.
3. The volatility of the underlying stock or futures price.
4. The time left until the expiration date of the option.
5. The short-term interest rate.

These five factors are the key determinants of the price of an option, and most of this information can be found in most major daily newspapers, except for measurement of price volatility. However, we have a special section in OPTION MASTER® for measuring volatility quite easily using the data that is available in the daily newspaper. Therefore, with your newspaper in hand, you can easily determine the fair price (true worth) of most options quickly.

WHERE TO START

Most investors approach the options markets by first finding a stock or commodity that they think is ready to move, and then look to the options market to pick an option. However, if you prefer to play the market as a whole, when you think the stock market is going to move up, you can choose an index, such as the S & P 100 (OEX) Index, and then select a call option on that index, hoping to participate if the whole market moves up in price.

Here your goal should be to select the best priced option that is available for the underlying stock, index or commodity that you like, and if all the options are overpriced, you should pass, and move on.

Option writers should be doing the opposite. If they want to write (sell) options, they should try to select the most overpriced options, and they should pass up stocks or commodities where all the options are underpriced.

Another approach to the options market that is a little bit unorthodox – rather than picking the stocks, commodities or futures in the market and then looking at their options, first try to find the most underpriced options by using OPTION MASTER®, and then from there, select the best stock or commodity. In this instance, by choosing underpriced options, you have stacked the odds in your favor to begin with, and now all you have to do is to identify an underlying instrument that has a good probability of moving in the right direction.

CHAPTER 2 - GETTING STARTED

OPTION MASTER® FOR WINDOWS™

Software Requirements

OPTION MASTER® for Windows™ requires Windows 3.0 or higher.

Installation for Version 1.3

OPTION MASTER® is supplied to you on a 3.5” disk. You MUST install the program to your hard drive. The INSTALL program will automatically load the program onto the C: drive in directory \OPMASTER.

To install the program, insert the OPTION MASTER® disk in Drive A. Move to drive A by typing “A:” and pressing “Enter.” Type INSTALL and press “Enter.” The program will now be installed to C:\OPMASTER.

Installation for Version 1.41

This version requires Windows 3.1 or higher. To install, insert disk in Drive A. From the *Program Manager,* choose *File, Run,* and then type A:\SETUP. To run the OPTION MASTER® program, click on the OPTION MASTER® icon.

Getting Started

To run OPTION MASTER®, log to your hard drive to the OPMASTER Directory. This would be C:cd OPMASTER. Then type WIN OM and press "Enter."

If Windows is already running, double click the *File Manager* (the File Cabinet Icon), click the proper drive and directory, and double click on the program OM.EXE.

To start the program using an icon, follow your Windows User's Guide instructions to establish an icon. These instructions include moving to "Windows Setup," then "Options," and then "Setup Applications."

Once you start running the program, there will be three menu items in the main menu bar. They include FILE, CALCULATE and EXTRAS.

FILE	Within this menu item, you can create a data file, open a previously saved file, or print the current window.
CALCULATE	Gives you a menu of the different screens and tasks that can be completed with OPTION MASTER® for Windows™.
EXTRAS	Here you are able to reconfigure your output screen, specify the startup screen and change the Multiple Strike Price increment value. In addition, you can delete files, and the "Help" section is under this menu item.

Moving Around the Screen

The key to using OPTION MASTER® for Windows™ is the TAB key (➔). Use the Tab Key to move from one entry box to another.

If you do not have a mouse, use the ALT key and the underline letter of the menu item you are selecting.

Calculate

By selecting *Calculate* on your menu bar, you will see a menu of the different screens and different tasks that can be completed with OPTION MASTER® for Windows™. This category has four major menu items: PRICES, PROBABILITIES, RATIOS and VOLATILITY.

Prices

This section of OPTION MASTER® for Windows™ calculates the theoretical prices for stock, index and commodity options.

Single Option Price

The menu item *Single Option Price* calculates the theoretical price of a stock or index option. Just enter the expiration month, stock or index price, strike price, volatility and the interest rate (3-month T Bill rate) in the appropriate entry boxes. Then click either *Put* or *Call* and you will see in the *Message Center* the theoretical put or call price, plus your probability of profit if you bought the option at the theoretical price, and the Delta. To change the date or year, click the "Arrow" or use the up and down arrow keys on your keyboard.

Multiple Option Prices

This menu screen calculates a whole range of theoretical option prices for a specific stock or index. Again, move from one entry box to another using the Tab key. When you reach the *Beginning Strike Price,* enter the lowest strike price that you wish to use. Then select the *Ending Strike Price.* Select the highest strike price for which you want to calculate option prices by clicking on the "arrow."

When selecting *Expiration Cycle,* if you select *Every Month,* OPTION MASTER® for Windows™ calculates the theoretical option prices for the next three months for the range of strike prices you have given. If you select the Jan, Apr, Jul, Oct cycle, OPTION MASTER® for Windows™ will calculate option prices for the three most recent upcoming months listed.

For example, in March, option prices would be calculated with expirations in April, July and October.

Commodity Option Prices

Calculating theoretical values for futures and commodity options is similar to stock or index options. The major difference is that you must enter the exact expiration date for the option contract.

Probabilities

Probability of Profit

This section of OPTION MASTER® for Windows™ calculates your probability of profit if you buy or sell (write) an option or enter an option strategy.

The *Probability of Profit* modules are similar to the option pricing modules, except that you must give the specific option price or break-even price (or stop-loss price) for a strategy. Again, move from one entry box to another using the TAB key.

Ratios

This section of OPTION MASTER® for Windows™ calculates the *Delta, Gamma, Theta* and *Vega* for a stock, index or futures option price.

All of these ratios can be calculated and automatically displayed when you calculate the theoretical price for an option by using the *Configure* menu item.

DELTA – is the percent of a point that the theoretical value of an option will change for a one-point change in the underlying stock, index or futures. For example, if a call stock option has a Delta of .50, the stock option will move up 1/2 of a point for every point that the stock moves up one point.

GAMMA – is the amount the Delta will change if the underlying stock index or futures changes one point. For example, if the Delta is .50 and the Gamma is .10, if the stock price increases by one point, the Delta will increase to .60 (.50 + .10 = .60).

THETA – is the time decay factor and is the rate at which an option will lose value as each day passes. For example, a Theta of .33 indicates that an option price will decrease in value .33 of a point as each day passes.

VEGA – is the point change in the theoretical value of an option for a one percentage point change in volatility. For example, if an option has a Vega of .50 to each percentage point increase in volatility, the option will gain 1/2 of a point.

Volatility

This section calculates both historical volatility and implied volatility. *Historical volatility* is the price volatility of a stock, index or futures based on past prices of the underlying instrument. Historical volatility is the most important component of the pricing model.

Implied volatility is the volatility as measured by the present price of the option in the options market. This volatility is what the market thinks the volatility should be.

Historical Volatility

When using the *Historical Volatility* menu screen, first select the *Observation Period.* We suggest "weekly observations."

Once you have entered the *Observation Period,* you can begin entering stock, index or futures prices for the past days, weeks or months. For example, if you have selected "Week," you could enter a stock's closing price for the past 10 or 20 weeks. Hit the Return or Tab key to enter each entry. You can calculate volatility any time by clicking the *Calculate Volatility* box.

Of course, you can edit the prices you have entered by clicking the *Add, Insert* and *Delete* boxes. If you wish to remove a price from the list, you mark the price by clicking on it with your mouse and then click the *Delete* box. To insert a price, do the same by marking the point at which you wish to insert a price, but now click the *Insert* box after you have entered a stock index or futures price at *Stock or Futures Price* entry location.

Once you have entered a series of prices, you can save those prices in a file by selecting *File* in the menu bar. So, you can add or update your specific stock or index files periodically and hence their volatilities.

Implied Volatility

When calculating *Implied Volatility,* you must provide the present market price for the option in question. Implied volatility is necessary for "what if" analysis. For example, if you want to find out what an option will be priced at if the stock moves accordingly, you will need the future date and the implied volatility. Then the Prices section of OPTION MASTER® for Windows™ will tell you the likely price of the option in the market.

OPTION MASTER® FOR DOS

Installation

OPTION MASTER® for DOS is supplied to you on a 3.5" disk. You can run OPTION MASTER® directly from Drive A or Drive B by typing MASTER and pressing ENTER. To install OPTION MASTER® to your hard drive, type INSTALL from the A or B drive, and provide a sub-directory where you wish to install OPTION MASTER®. For example, at the A drive-A>, type INSTALL C:\OPMASTER and press the ENTER key. Then the program will automatically set up OPTION MASTER® on the C-Drive in sub-directory OPMASTER.

Getting Started

To run OPTION MASTER®, log to your hard drive to the OPMASTER directory, if you use this directory. This would be C:cd OPMASTER. Then type MASTER and press ENTER.

Once you start running the program, there will be three menu items in the main menu bar. They include FILE, CALCULATE and EXTRAS.

FILE	Within this menu item, you can create a data file, open a previously saved file, or print the current window.
CALCULATE	Gives you a menu of the different screens and tasks that can be completed with OPTION MASTER® for DOS.
EXTRAS	Here you are able to reconfigure your output screen, specify the startup screen and change the Multiple Strike Price increment value. In addition, you can delete files, and the "Help" section is under this menu item.

Moving Around the Screen

The key to using OPTION MASTER® for DOS is the TAB key (➔). Use the Tab Key to move from one entry box to another.

If you do not have a mouse, use the ALT key and the underline letter of the menu item you are selecting. Press the ALT key to identify the proper letter to press.

ALT Commands

Main Menu

ALT + F	File
ALT + A	Calculate

Calculate Menu

ALT + P	Put Prices
ALT + C	Call Prices

Extras Menu

ALT + D	Delete Data Files
ALT + C	Custom

Configure Menu

ALT + D	Default
ALT + C	Custom
ALT + A	Always
ALT + W	When Called from Menu
ALT + P	Puts
ALT + C	Calls
ALT + I	Ignore

Calculate

By selecting *Calculate* on your menu bar, you will see a menu of the different screens and different tasks that can be completed with OPTION MASTER® for DOS. This category has four major menu items: PRICES, PROBABILITIES, RATIOS and VOLATILITY.

Prices

This section of OPTION MASTER® for DOS calculates the theoretical prices for stock, index and commodity options.

Single Option Price

The menu item *Single Option Price* calculates the theoretical price of a stock or index option. Just enter the *Expiration Month, Stock or Index Price, Strike Price, Volatility* and the *Interest Rate* (3-month T Bill rate) in the appropriate entry boxes. Then click either *Put* or *Call* and you will see in the *Message Center* the theoretical put or call price, plus your probability of profit if you bought the option at the theoretical price, and the Delta. To change the date or year, click the "Arrow" or use the up and down arrow keys on your keyboard.

Multiple Option Prices

This menu screen calculates a whole range of theoretical option prices for a specific stock or index. Again, move from one entry box to another using the Tab key. When you reach the *Low Strike Price,* enter the lowest strike price that you wish to use.

When selecting *Expiration Cycle,* if you select *Every Month,* OPTION MASTER® for DOS calculates the theoretical option prices for the next three months for the range of strike prices you have given. If you select the Jan, Apr, Jul, Oct cycle, OPTION MASTER® for DOS will calculate option prices for the three most recent upcoming months listed.

For example, in March, option prices would be calculated with expirations in April, July and October.

Commodity Option Prices

Calculating theoretical values for futures and commodity

options is similar to stock or index options, with a few differences that are discussed in the next chapter.

Probabilities

Probability of Profit

This section of OPTION MASTER® for DOS calculates your probability of profit if you buy or sell (write) an option or enter an option strategy.

The *Probability of Profit* modules are similar to the option pricing modules, except that you must give the specific option price or break-even price (or stop-loss price) for a strategy. Again, move from one entry box to another using the Tab key.

Ratios

This section of OPTION MASTER® for DOS calculates the *Delta, Gamma, Theta* and *Vega* for a stock, index or futures option price.

All of these ratios can be calculated and automatically displayed when you calculate the theoretical price for an option by using the *Configure* menu item.

> **DELTA** – is the percent of a point that the theoretical value of an option will change for a one-point change in the underlying stock, index or futures. For example, if a call stock option has a Delta of .50, the stock option will move up 1/2 of a point for every point that the stock moves up one point.

GAMMA – is the amount the Delta will change if the underlying stock index or futures changes one point. For example, if the Delta is .50 and the Gamma is .10, if the stock price increases by one point, the Delta will increase to .60 (.50 + .10 = .60).

THETA – is the time decay factor and is the rate at which an option will lose value as each day passes. For example, a Theta of .33 indicates that an option price will decrease in value .33 of a point as each day passes.

VEGA – is the point change in the theoretical value of an option for a one percentage point change in volatility. For example, if an option has a Vega of .50 to each percentage point increase in volatility, the option will gain 1/2 of a point.

Volatility

This section calculates both historical volatility and implied volatility. *Historical volatility* is the price volatility of a stock, index or futures based on past prices of the underlying instrument. Historical volatility is the most important component of the pricing model.

Implied volatility is the volatility as measured by the present price of the option in the options market. This volatility is what the market thinks the volatility should be.

Historical Volatility

When using the *Historical Volatility* menu screen, first select the *Observation Period.* We suggest "weekly observations."

Once you have entered the *Observation Period,* you can begin entering stock, index or futures prices for the past days, weeks or months. For example, if you have selected *Week,* you could enter a stock's closing price for the past 10 or 20 weeks. Hit the Return or Tab key to enter each entry. You can calculate volatility any time by clicking the *Calculate Volatility* box.

Of course, you can edit the prices you have entered by clicking the *Add, Insert* and *Delete* boxes. If you wish to remove a price from the list, you mark the price by clicking on it with your mouse and then click the *Delete* box. To insert a price, do the same by marking the point at which you wish to insert a price, but now click the *Insert* box after you have entered a stock index or futures price at *Stock or Futures Price* entry location.

Once you have entered a series of prices, you can save those prices in a file by selecting *File* in the menu bar. So, you can add or update your specific stock or index files periodically and hence their volatilities.

Implied Volatility

When calculating *Implied Volatility,* you must provide the present market price for the option in question. Implied volatility is necessary for "what if" analysis. For example, if you want to find out what an option will be priced at if the stock moves accordingly, you will need the future date and the implied volatility. Then the *Prices* section of OPTION MASTER® for DOS will tell you the likely price of the option in the market.

OPTION MASTER® ON THE MACINTOSH®

Installation

OPTION MASTER® can be run from the disk supplied to you by clicking on the OPTION MASTER® icon, or you can install OPTION MASTER® by dragging the OPTION MASTER® icon to your hard drive.

The Menu

The key to using the Macintosh version of OPTION MASTER® is the TAB key (➔). Use the Tab Key to move from one menu item to another.

By selecting *Calculate Price* on your menu bar, you will see a menu of the different screens and different tasks that can be completed with OPTION MASTER®.

Single Option Price

The menu item *Single Option Price* calculates the theoretical price of a stock or index option. Just enter the *Expiration Month, Stock or Index Price, Strike Price* and the *Volatility* in the appropriate entry boxes. Then click either *Put* or *Call* and you will see in the *Message Center* the theoretical put or call price, plus your probability of profit if you bought the option at the theoretical price.

Multiple Option Prices

This menu screen calculates a whole range of theoretical option prices for a specific stock or index. Again, move from one menu item to another using the Tab key. When you reach the *Beginning Strike Price,* enter the lowest strike price that you wish to use. Then select from the range of prices available for *Ending Strike Price.* Select the highest strike price for which you want to calculate option prices.

When selecting *Expiration Cycle,* if you select *Every Month,* OPTION MASTER® will calculate the theoretical option prices for the next three months for the range of strike prices you have given. If you select the Jan, Apr, Jul, Oct cycle, OPTION MASTER® will calculate option prices for the three most recent upcoming months listed.

For example, in March, option prices would be calculated with expirations in April, July and October.

Calculate Volatility

When using the *Calculate Volatility* menu screen, first select the *Observation Period.* We suggest "weekly observations."

Once you have entered the *Observation Period,* you can begin entering stock, index or futures prices for the past days, weeks or months. For example, if you have selected *Week,* you could enter a stock's closing price for the past 10 or 20 weeks. Hit the Return or Tab key to enter each entry. You can calculate volatility any time by clicking the *Calculate Volatility* box.

Of course, you can edit the prices you have entered by clicking the *Add, Insert* and *Delete* boxes. If you wish to remove a price from the list, you mark the price by clicking on it with your mouse and then click the *Delete* box. To insert a price, do the same by marking the point at which you wish to insert a price, but now click the *Insert* box after you have entered a stock index or futures price at *Stock or Futures Price* entry location.

Once you have entered a series of prices, you can save those prices in a file by selecting *File* in the menu bar. So, you can add or update your specific stock, index or commodity files periodically and hence their volatilities.

Commodity Option Prices

Calculating theoretical values for futures and commodity options is similar to stock or index options, with a few differences that are discussed in the next chapter.

Probability of Profit

The *Probability of Profit* modules are similar to the option pricing modules, except that you must give the specific option price or break-even price (or stop loss price) for a strategy. Again, move from one menu item to another using the Tab key. The use of the *Probability of Profit* module is discussed in the next chapter.

OPTION MASTER® FOR NEWTON™

Requirements

If you purchased a storage card with OPTION MASTER® in place, you only need a Newton™ computer device. Without this storage card, you will need a Macintosh computer running System 7, or you will need an IBM PC-compatible computer running Windows 3.1 or higher and the Newton Connection Kit.

Installation

If OPTION MASTER® is already on your storage card, just insert the storage card in your Newton™ and you are ready to get started. If you are using a Macintosh, connect your Newton-compatible device to your computer with a serial cable, or the Newton Connection Kit cable. Insert the appropriate disk (when using the Newton Connection Kit). Launch the Newton Package Installer, or if you are using the Newton Connection Kit, select Install Package from the Newton menu. Then select OPTION MASTER®. (With an IBM PC using the Newton Connection Kit, follow the same procedure.)

Then immediately choose *Connection* from the *Extras* drawer on your Newton-compatible device, then select *Macintosh Serial* or *DOS* or *Windows PC* and press the *Connect* button. After a few minutes, OPTION MASTER® will be installed on your Newton-compatible device.

Getting Started

After installing OPTION MASTER®, the program will appear in the *Extras* drawer. Tap on its picture to start the program. Once you start, the *Stock/Index Option Price* screen will appear. This screen will calculate stock and index option prices.

TAPPING and WRITING

The OPTION MASTER® for Newton™ program is designed to minimize the amount of writing on the Newton screen and maximize the amount of "tapping" to activate menu items or enter data. For example, *Beginning Date* can be changed by tapping on the black diamond to the left of *Beg. Date.*

Now you are given a choice of the 12 months. Just Tap the month you desire. To change the day of the month, just Tap the "up" or "down" arrow to the right of the date. The same procedure applies to change the year.

The only writing that is usually needed is to change the stock, index or futures price. You do this by scrubbing out the previous price and writing in the new stock price. To enter the fraction for a stock price, just Tap on the *Stock Price.* You will be given the range of fractions to choose from. Tap on your choice.

To enter the *Strike Price,* just Tap on the words *Strike Price* and you will be given the range of strike prices to choose from. Tap on your selection. If the strike price you desire is not available, you can write in the desired strike price. To enter *Volatility,* the same procedure is followed. However, when you Tap on *Volatility,* you will first be given a range of volatilities to select from (i.e., 1–10 or 11–20). If the volatility you desire is 16%, Tap on "11–20" and then Tap on 16. If the volatility you desire is not on the list, you can write it in. Whenever an item in the program has a diamond before it, you can Tap on it and get a range of choices from the menu.

Calculate

By tapping on *Calculate* at the top of the Newton screen, you will see a menu of the different screens and different tasks that can be completed with OPTION MASTER® for Newton™. This category has four major menu items: P*rices, Probabilities, Ratios* and *Volatility.*

Prices

This section of OPTION MASTER® for Newton™ calculates the theoretical prices for stock, index and commodity options.

Stock/Index Option Price

The menu item, **Stock/Index Option Price,** calculates the theoretical price of a stock or index option. Just enter the *Expiration Month, Stock or Index Price, Strike Price, Volatility* and the *Interest Rate* (3-month T Bill rate) as indicated. Then Tap either *Put* or *Call* and you will see in the *Message Center* the theoretical put or call price, plus your probability of profit if you bought the option at the theoretical price, and the *Delta.* The *End Date* usually refers to the "Expiration Date."

Multiple Option Prices

This menu screen calculates an entire range of theoretical options for a specific stock or index. By tapping the *Low Strike*

Price, you are specifying the option with the lowest strike price that you wish to calculate.

Commodity Option Prices

Here you Tap either *Grains, Bonds* or *Other Commodities* for other commodities and other futures contracts. Calculating theoretical values for futures and commodity options is similar to stock or index options, with a few differences that are discussed in the next chapter.

Multiple Futures Prices

This menu screen calculates a whole range of theoretical option prices for a specific futures contract.

Probabilities

Probability of Profit

This section of OPTION MASTER® for Newton™ calculates your probability of profit if you buy or sell (write) an option or enter an option strategy.

The *Probability of Profit* modules are similar to the option pricing modules, except that you must give the specific option price or break-even price (or stop-loss price) for a strategy.

Ratios

This section of OPTION MASTER® for Newton™ calculates the *Delta, Gamma, Theta* and *Vega* for a stock, index or futures option price.

DELTA – is the percent of a point that the theoretical value of an option will change for a one-point change in the underlying stock, index or futures. For example, if a call stock option has a Delta of .50, the stock option will move up 1/2 of a point for every point that the stock moves up one point.

GAMMA – is the amount the Delta will change if the underlying stock index or futures changes one point. For example, if the Delta is .50 and the Gamma is .10, if the stock price increases by one point, the Delta will increase to .60 (.50 + .10 = .60).

THETA – is the time decay factor and is the rate at which an option will lose value as each day passes. For example, a Theta of .33 indicates that an option price will decrease in value .33 of a point as each day passes.

VEGA – is the point change in the theoretical value of an option for a one percentage point change in volatility. For example, if an option has a Vega of .50 to each percentage point increase in volatility, the option will gain 1/2 of a point.

Volatility

This section calculates both historical volatility and implied volatility. *Historical volatility* is the price volatility of a stock, index or futures based on past prices of the underlying instrument. Historical volatility is the most important component of the pricing model.

Implied volatility is the volatility as measured by the present price of the option in the options market. This volatility is what the market thinks the volatility should be.

Historical Volatility

When using the *Historical Volatility* menu screen, first select the *Observation Period.* We suggest "weekly observations."

Once you have entered the *Observation Period,* you can begin entering stock, index or futures prices for the past days, weeks or months. For example, if you have selected *Weekly,* you could enter a stock's closing price for the past 10 or 20 weeks. To enter prices, write the first stock, index or futures price in next to the diamond under *Price.* Then Tap the *Add* box. The price will be placed in the screen below. Try to avoid entering prices with fractions or decimals to speed up the entry process. You will usually not lose much by rounding off your prices unless you are working with Bonds or T-Bills or similar instruments where fractions are important.

After you have entered the first price and added it to the list, you only need to Tap on the diamond next to the price and you will be given a menu of prices to choose from by tapping on the numbers. This will enable you to avoid writing in additional numbers. To delete a number from the list, just scrub it out. To insert a number in the list, enter the number you wish to insert, then Tap on the insert box and Tap on the price in the list below the position you wish to insert the new price. Once you have entered past prices for several weeks or months, just Tap on the *Calculate* box to calculate volatility.

Implied Volatility

When calculating implied volatility, you must provide the present market price for the option in question. Implied volatility is necessary for "what if" analysis. For example, if you want to find out what an option will be priced at if the stock moves accordingly, you will need the future date and the implied volatility. Then the Prices section of OPTION MASTER® for Newton™ will tell you the likely price of the option in the market.

Entry Tips

When entering commodity and futures prices, avoid decimals if possible (i.e., instead of 60.5, use 605); and due to the wide variety of strike prices for futures, you may need to write in your own strike prices because the strike price you desire will not be available on the strike price menu.

If the Newton™ has trouble recognizing the number you write, just scrub it out and Tap twice. The Newton™ will give a calculator on the screen. Now you can quickly Tap in the number with ease.

CHAPTER 3
USING OPTION MASTER®

QUICK AND EASY

The OPTION MASTER® computer program is designed to quickly price options for you with few entries, and it is designed for great ease in use. After fifteen to thirty minutes of practice, you will discover OPTION MASTER® to be easy-to-use and understand and you probably will rarely have to resort to reading this manual after a few sessions of practice.

The goal of our program is to allow you to enter the fewest key strokes possible so that you can quickly price many options within a short period of time, or determine your probability of profit when you buy or sell an option or enter an option strategy.

In addition, there is a volatility calculation so that you can calculate the price volatility for the underlying stock, index or commodity futures contract, which is one of the required inputs in this program.

A PRACTICE SESSION

To demonstrate the features of OPTION MASTER®, we will walk through several examples using the different features of OPTION MASTER®. The figures used are from OPTION MASTER® for Windows™. OPTION MASTER® for DOS is identical to OPTION MASTER® for Windows™, except for slight differences in graphics. The current version of OPTION MASTER® for Macintosh® also operates in a similar fashion to OPTION MASTER® for Windows™, but does not include all of the OPTION MASTER® for Windows™ features.

Pricing An Option

Let's assume that you wish to determine the fair Theoretical Value for a call option on a specific stock, such as IBM, in this case, the IBM September 110 call, with IBM priced at 105 3/8, with the present date being August 5, 1995. For a single stock or index price, go to the menu item, "Single Option Price." You can do this by clicking on *Calculate,* then *Prices* and finally *Single Option Price.* There are six entries that are required:

1. Beginning Date (today's date)
2. Expiration Month
3. Stock Price (stock or index price)
4. Strike Price
5. Volatility
6. Interest Rate (3-month Treasury Bill rate)

The Beginning Date is usually today's date, and your computer should default automatically to that date. Now, using the tab key, move to *Expiration Month.* You can select the month by clicking on the "arrow" or using the arrow keys, or by just typing the first letter of the month.

Now move to the *Stock Price* entry box using the tab key. Enter the IBM stock price, 105 3/8. You may use the decimal instead of a fraction if you wish (i.e., 105.37). Now move to the *Strike Price* entry box and enter the strike price of 110.

Next, tab to the *Volatility* entry box. Volatility (the amount the price will move up or down within a specific time span) refers to the historical price volatility of the underlying stock, index or commodity. OPTION MASTER® will calculate the Historical

Volatility in the *Volatility* menu item of the program *(refer to Chapter 4).*

As a rule of thumb, you can enter .30 for a stock with average price volatility, .20 for a stock with low price volatility, and .45 for a stock with high price volatility.

Broad-based indexes have price volatilities that range from .07 to .15. These volatilities are quoted in percents, so .07 is 7%.

Commodity and other futures contracts vary dramatically. For example, Treasury Bonds usually have a volatility of around 8%. Currencies usually have volatilities from 5% to 13%. Treasury Bills or Eurodollars have a volatility of between 1% and 2%. The volatility for grains usually ranges from 10% to 40%, pork bellies 30% to 40%, gold 10% to 20%, silver 20% to 30%. *(Refer to Chapter 4 for typical volatilities.)*

With our IBM example, we use a volatility of 30%, or .30. The program always defaults to this volatility.

Finally, using the Tab key, move to the Interest Rate entry box and enter the 3-month Treasury Bill rate, or the prevailing short-term interest rate (i.e., 5% = .05).

Now you are ready to calculate the fair Theoretical Price for the IBM September 110 call. Just click on the Call Prices box and the results will be displayed in the Message Center. *(Refer to Figure 2)*

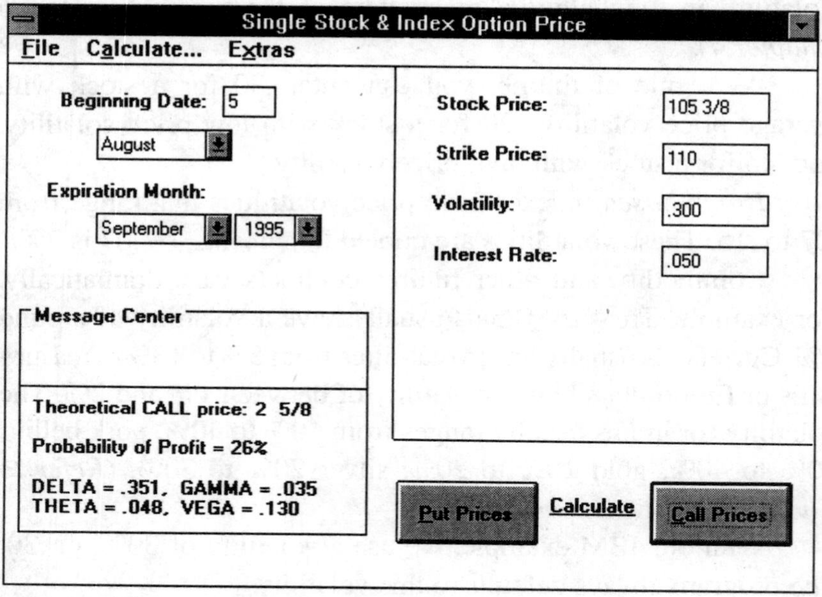

Single Stock & Index Option Price

File Calculate... Extras

Beginning Date: 5
August

Expiration Month:
September 1995

Stock Price: 105 3/8
Strike Price: 110
Volatility: .300
Interest Rate: .050

Message Center

Theoretical CALL price: 2 5/8
Probability of Profit = 26%
DELTA = .351, GAMMA = .035
THETA = .048, VEGA = .130

Put Prices Calculate Call Prices

Figure 2

As you can see, the Theoretical Call Price is 2 5/8. Your Probability of Profit, if you purchased this option at its theoretical price, is 26% if held until expiration. If you are an option writer, your Probability of Profit would be the inverse of this figure. In other words, you subtract the 26% from 100%, giving you a Probability of Profit of 74% (100 - 26 = 74).

OPTION MASTER® also displays the Delta, Gamma, Theta and Vega that are defined in *Chapter 2.* Once you have the theoretical price for an option, you can compare it to the actual price in the market through the newspaper, your quote system, or your broker.

PRICING SEVERAL OPTIONS

Now let's say that you want to determine the theoretical price for a whole group of options for three expiration months. Let's use the S & P 500 Index (SPX) options in this example with the SPX at 559.02 and a volatility of 11%.

First click on *Calculate,* then select *Prices* and then select *Multiple Option Prices.* On the *Multiple Stock & Index Option Prices* screen, *Beginning Date* is again today's date, here August 5, 1995. Clicking on the arrow next to the *Expiration Cycle* gives you the choice of "every month" – the next three months, or the months in the January expiration cycle, the February expiration cycle, or the March expiration cycle. We will select *Every Month.* Next to *Stock Price,* enter the S & P 500 Index price of 559.06. The *Beginning Strike Price* requires the lowest strike price that you want to determine option value. Enter 540 in this entry box. Tab to *Ending Strike Price* and using the arrow key, select a strike price of 575 – the highest strike price on which you wish to price options. Tab to *Volatility* and enter .11. Then tab to *Interest Rate* and enter .05. Always make sure to tab out of an entry box before doing a calculation.

Now by clicking on *Put Prices* (or *Call Prices*), you receive a whole range of theoretical option prices. (*Refer to Figures 3 and 4)*

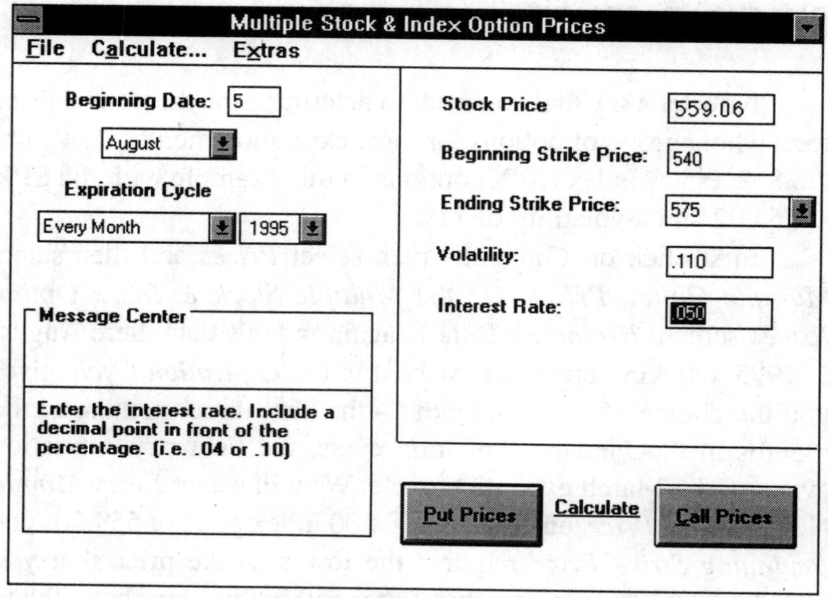

Figure 3

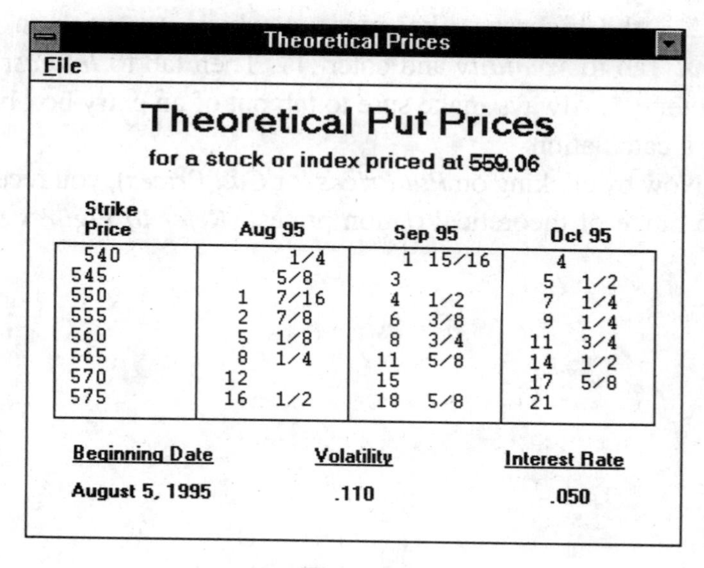
Theoretical Prices

File

Theoretical Put Prices

for a stock or index priced at 559.06

Strike Price	Aug 95	Sep 95	Oct 95
540	1/4	1 15/16	4
545	5/8	3	5 1/2
550	1 7/16	4 1/2	7 1/4
555	2 7/8	6 3/8	9 1/4
560	5 1/8	8 3/4	11 3/4
565	8 1/4	11 5/8	14 1/2
570	12	15	17 5/8
575	16 1/2	18 5/8	21

Beginning Date	Volatility	Interest Rate
August 5, 1995	.110	.050

Figure 4

This table of theoretical index put option prices in *Figure 4* can then be printed for future reference.

CALCULATING FUTURES OPTIONS PRICES

Entries to determine the theoretical price for a *commodity* option differ in several aspects from pricing *stock* options. First, you must enter the exact date that the futures option expires.

The options on a specific commodity expire at a different time in the month than other commodity options, usually in the previous month to the futures contract. You can obtain a calendar that spells out the expiration date for each set of futures options from your commodity broker. Such a calendar is also published in *Futures* magazine.

When entering the futures price and strike price, make sure to follow the example that accompanies the computer prompts. When entering grain prices such as wheat, corn or soybeans, enter the price as cents, rather than dollars and *cents.* For example, if September wheat is priced at $4.01 a bushel, enter 401 – *not* 4.01. When entering prices for other commodities such as hogs or cattle, enter the cents per pound as a whole number. For example, if September hogs are priced at 49.23¢, enter the price as 49.23, *not* .4923. Currencies would also be entered as whole numbers for cents. For example, if the Japanese Yen is priced at .6824 per 100 Yen, enter 68.24 – *do not* enter .6824.

When entering *strike* prices, follow the same format and be consistent. If you enter 400 for the futures price and 4.00 for the strike price, the theoretical option price would be way out-of-line. Therefore, rather than give you a faulty price, the program gives you an error message.

Entering *bond* prices is different than other futures contracts. You enter bond prices in points and 32nds. Therefore, to enter 90 18/32, you would enter 90 18/32 or 90.18. OPTION MASTER® converts the 90.18 into 90 18/32 automatically.

ANOTHER PRACTICE SESSION

Let's determine the fair theoretical value of the Soybean November 650 call on August 3, 1995, with the Soybeans November futures contract priced at 608.5. First click *Calculate,* then select *Prices.* Then select *Grains* under the heading *Commodity Option Prices.*

The *Beginning Date* is again today's date. Tab to *Expiration Date* and type in the expiration date, which in this case is October 20, 1995. Again, to select the month, tab to it and just type in the first letter of the month or use the arrow key.

Now tab to the *Futures Price* and enter 608.5. Tab to *Strike Price* and enter 650. Tab to *Volatility* and enter the historical price volatility for the Soybeans futures contract. *(Refer to Chapter 4 to determine volatility.)*

Presently, we will use a volatility of 40%, or .40. So enter .40 in the *Volatility* entry box. Tab to *Interest Rate* and enter the 3-month Treasury Bill rate (i.e., .05 for 5%). Then tab out of this box. Always tab out of an entry box where you have made a change before activating a calculation. Now you are ready to calculate the theoretical price of the Soybeans call. Click on *Call Prices* and check the *Message Center* for the results. *(See Figure 5)*

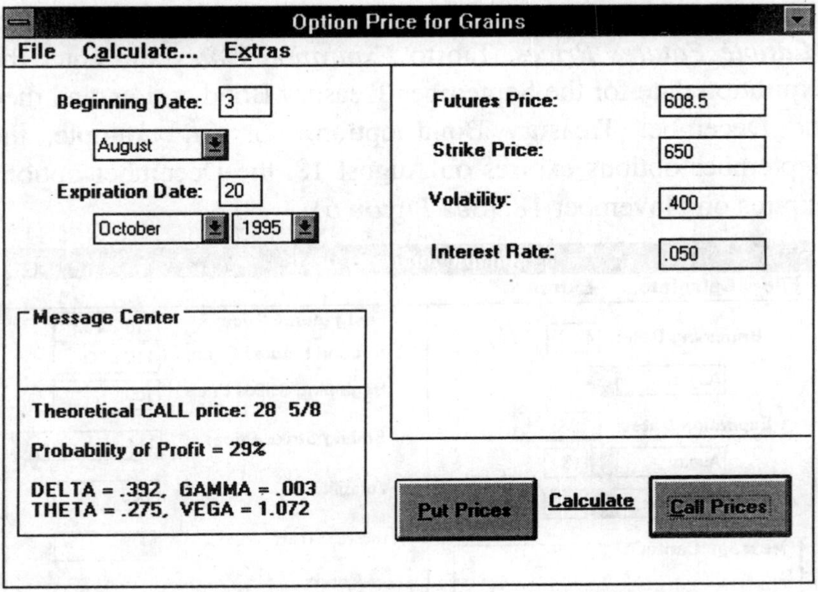

Option Price for Grains

File Calculate... Extras

Beginning Date: 3 August

Expiration Date: 20 October 1995

Futures Price: 608.5

Strike Price: 650

Volatility: .400

Interest Rate: .050

Message Center

Theoretical CALL price: 28 5/8

Probability of Profit = 29%

DELTA = .392, GAMMA = .003
THETA = .275, VEGA = 1.072

Put Prices Calculate Call Prices

Figure 5

As you can see, the theoretical Soybean call price is 28 5/8¢, and your probability of profit of 29%, if you buy the option at its theoretical price and hold until expiration. If you are an option writer, your probability of profit would be the inverse of 29%. In other words, 29% subtracted from 100%, giving you a Probability of Profit of 71% (100 - 29 = 71).

Multiple Futures Options

You can also determine the theoretical price on a whole series of futures options. Let's use Treasury Bonds to demonstrate this feature.

We will determine the theoretical price for a series of options on the September and December Treasury Bond futures contracts.

Click on *Calculate* in the menu bar. Select *Prices,* and then select *Multiple Futures Prices.* Tab to *Expiration Dates* and enter the expiration date for the September Treasury Bond option, and then the December Treasury Bond option. For our example, the September options expires on August 18, the December options expires on November 18. *(See Figure 6).*

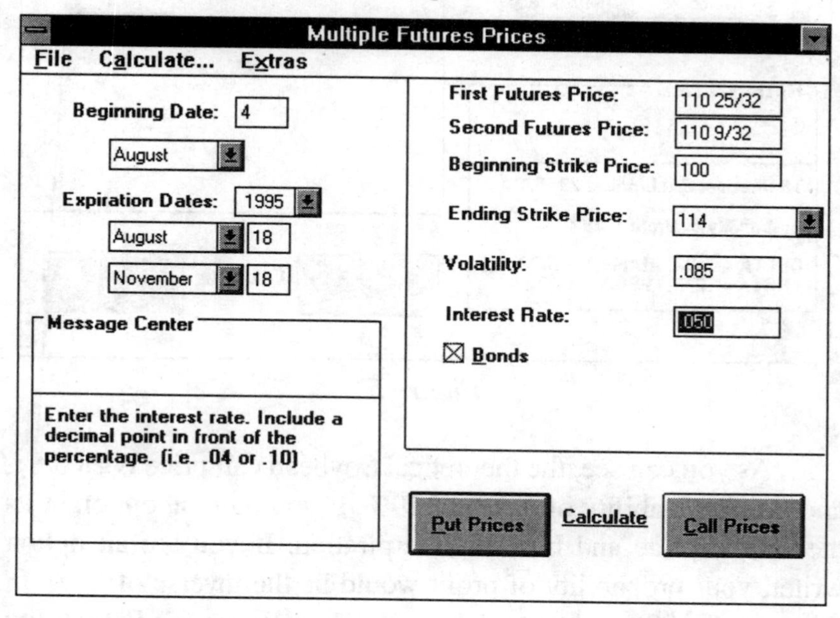

Figure 6

Now tab to the *First Futures Price* and enter the September Treasury Bond futures price for August 4, 1995 – 110 25/32. You enter this price as 110.25 and it will convert the decimal to a fraction – but first click the *Bond* box below with your mouse.

Now tab to the *Second Futures Price* and enter the December Treasury Bond futures contract price of 110 9/32, or 110.09.

Now tab to *Beginning Strike Price* and enter the lowest strike price on which you want to price options. Continue to *Ending Strike Price* and by using the arrow key, select the highest strike price you wish to use.

Strike prices for bonds are in 2-point increments. Therefore, you must change the increment rate. To do this, click *Extras* in the top menu bar. Select *Configure.* Under the category of *Multiple Strike Price Increment Value,* click *Custom* and Tab to the entry box and enter the number 2, and click *Save.*

In *Figure 6,* we used a low strike price of 100 and a high strike price of 114. Now Tab to *Volatility* and enter a volatility of 8.5%, or .085. Tab out of Volatility and click *Put Prices.*

Figure 7 shows the theoretical *Put Prices Table* generated by this calculation. By clicking on *File,* you can either print this table or return to the program. As you can see, Treasury Bond options are quoted in points and 64ths.

Theoretical Prices

File

Theoretical Put Prices

for a futures priced at 110 25/32 and 110 9/32

Strike Price	Aug 95	Nov 95	
100	0	2/64	
102	0	6/64	
104	0	15/64	
106	0	34/64	
108	4/64	1 4/64	
110	27/64	1 57/64	
112	1 32/64	3	
114	3 16/64	4 27/64	

Beginning Date	Volatility	Interest Rate
August 4, 1995	.085	.050

Figure 7

Other Commodities

When attempting to determine the theoretical value of a futures option other than a grain or bond – such as gold, silver, copper, the currencies, cattle, hogs, oil, etc. – select *Other Commodities* under the *Prices* menu.

Using Configure

Under the *Extras* menu in the top menu bar, select the item *Configure (see Figure 8).* As we saw when pricing Multiple Futures Options, you can change the increment value between strike prices – with stocks the typical increment is 5 points, but the Option Exchanges are now experimenting with 2 1/2 price increments. So as needed, you can change the increment you will use. In addition, you can decide to display the Delta, Gamma, Vega and Theta every time you price an option by selecting *Always.* You can also specify the *Startup Screen.*

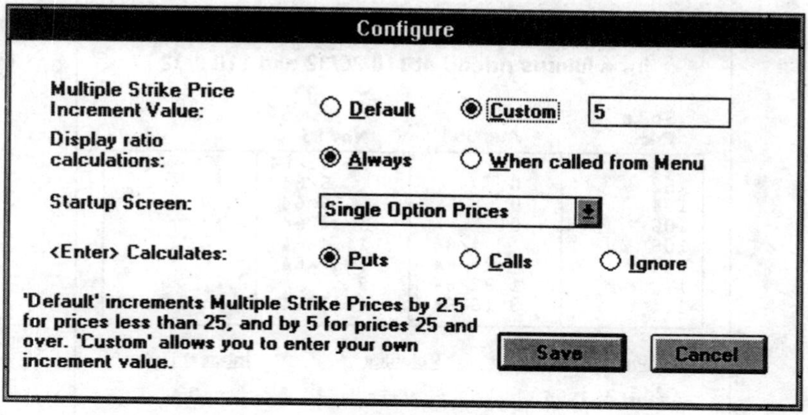

Configure

Multiple Strike Price Increment Value: Default / Custom [5]

Display ratio calculations: Always / When called from Menu

Startup Screen: Single Option Prices

<Enter> Calculates: Puts / Calls / Ignore

'Default' increments Multiple Strike Prices by 2.5 for prices less than 25, and by 5 for prices 25 and over. 'Custom' allows you to enter your own increment value.

Save Cancel

Figure 8

OPTION MASTER'S
FAIR PRICE LIST:
Intelligence on best Option Values
NEWSPAPER LISTINGS:
Actual Closing Option Prices.
FAIR PRICE
NEWSPAPER
OPTIONS

CHAPTER 4
THE NAME OF THE GAME IS VOLATILITY

The most important component in measuring the fair price for a stock, index or futures option is the price volatility of the underlying stock, index or future. In other words, the average amount the stock, index or futures price fluctuates up or down in a given time. Your measure of the underlying price volatility will be your determinant of how successfully you are able to measure the fair price for an option.

What you are trying to do is estimate the future volatility of the underlying stock, index or futures. You do this by determining the historical volatility of the underlying instrument. Historical volatility is defined as a standard deviation of a change in price as used in pricing models such as OPTION MASTER®.

There are several published sources where you can get the historical volatility for stocks, indexes and futures. For example, the historical volatility for almost 200 stocks are published in the *Trester Complete Option Report,* available from The Institute for Options Research, Inc., P.O. Box 6586, Lake Tahoe, Nevada 89449. Historical volatility for most option stocks, indexes and currencies are published in *Daily Graphs Option Guide,* P.O. Box 66919, Los Angeles, California 90066.

OPTION MASTER® will also calculate any historical volatility that you desire. Typical historical volatility ranges for stocks, indexes and futures contracts are presented in *Table I.*

Typical Volatility Ranges

Underlying Instrument	Volatility Range	Underlying Instrument	Volatility Range
Low Volatility Stocks	10% - 25%	Orange Juice	15% - 30%
Average Volatility Stocks	25% - 35%	Pork Bellies	25% - 40%
High Volatility Stocks	35% - 55%	Silver	15% - 30%
Broad Based Indexes	5% - 15%	Soybeans	20% - 35%
Cattle, Feeder	5% - 15%	Soybean Meal	20% - 35%
Cattle, Live	5% - 15%	Soybean Oil	20% - 35%
Cocoa	20% - 35%	Sugar	30% - 45%
Coffee	20% - 40%	Wheat	15% - 35%
Copper	20% - 35%	British pound	7% - 15%
Corn	30% - 35%	Canadian dollar	3.5% - 10%
Cotton	20% - 30%	Deutschemark	7% - 15%
Crude Oil	20% - 35%	Eurodollar	.8% - 2%
Gold	5% - 20%	Japanese yen	7% - 18%
Heating Oil	20% - 35%	Swiss franc	7% - 17%
Hogs	15% - 30%	T-bills	1% - 2.4%
Lumber	10% - 25%	T-bonds	7% - 12%

Table I

To calculate historical volatility, click on *Calculate* in the top menu bar, then select *Volatility* and then select *Historical Volatility.* Now you are in the *Calculate Volatility* screen.

To measure historical volatility, you need to enter past prices for the underlying stock, index or futures.

A quick and dirty way to calculate a historical volatility would be to enter the high and low price for the past year for a stock, index or commodity. But this historical volatility figure is crude and may be inaccurate. In fact, the more time you spend in measuring volatility, the more successful and accurate you will be in determining the true theoretical value for the options that you are reviewing.

To measure historical volatility, you first select the observation period by clicking on *Day, Week, Month* or *Year.* Market makers use a daily observation period using prices for each trading day. Usually, they are a 20 to 30-day history. One of the reasons that they use this period is because they hold option positions for very short periods of time. If you plan to hold an option position for a longer period of time, you should use a longer price history.

In our research, we found that a 20-week history with one observation period per week (the closing price on one day each week) showed a high correlation with the future volatility of the underlying stock, index or commodity.

SOME PRACTICE SESSIONS

Let's go through two examples to show you how to calculate historical volatility. The menu screen has been designed for ease of use, so you may quickly enter prices.

Let's say you wish to calculate the historical volatility for Microsoft. First, click on *Week.* The easiest way to enter data is by using a chart book with a chart of Microsoft, but old newspapers will also do the job. Select the Microsoft closing price for one day each week, starting with the earliest week. Try to be consistent using the same day each week. For example, we collected the past 10 weeks of price listings for Microsoft, one closing price per week. We started with 89 ten weeks ago, then 85, 84, 85, 91, 90, 92, 100, 95 and then 92. As you will notice, we dropped the fractions to allow for faster and easier entry. Adding the fractions will probably not add much to your accuracy.

Now begin entering these prices in the entry box, *Stock or Futures Price.* Hit the *Enter* or *Return* key after each entry.

Now click on *Calculate Volatility.* As you can see, the volatility is .311 (31.1%). *(See Figure 10)* You can calculate volatility at any time during the entry process as long as you have two entries or more. Now you can save this file by clicking on the *File* menu. Make sure that the files you save have the extension **.OMV,** so that they will be easy to retrieve.

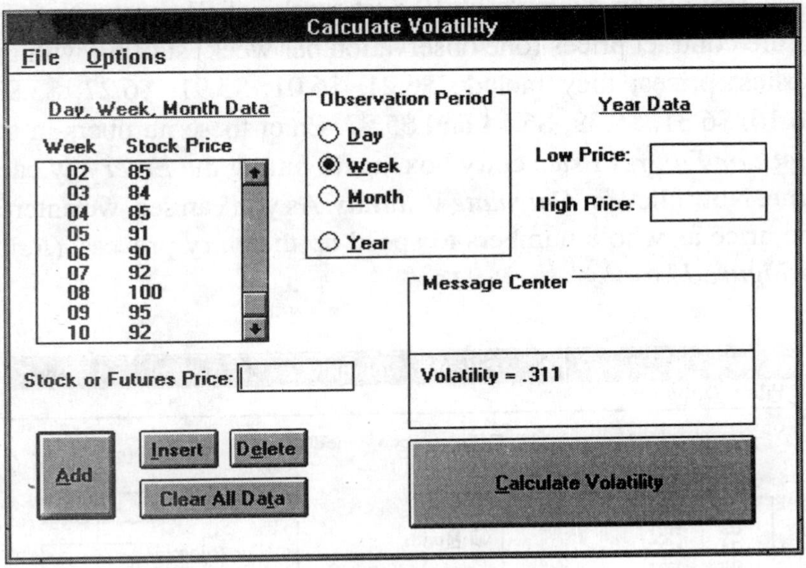

Calculate Volatility

File Options

Day, Week, Month Data

Week	Stock Price
02	85
03	84
04	85
05	91
06	90
07	92
08	100
09	95
10	92

Observation Period
Day
Week
Month
Year

Year Data
Low Price:
High Price:

Message Center
Volatility = .311

Stock or Futures Price:

Add
Insert
Delete
Clear All Data
Calculate Volatility

Figure 10

As you continue to update this file, you can delete previous prices (i.e., beyond 20 weeks) by clicking the *Delete* button after selecting the price you wish to delete. You also can insert prices by clicking on the stock price after the one you wish to insert and then clicking the *Insert* button. Make sure you have typed in a price before clicking the *Insert* button.

Now let's calculate the volatility for a soybeans futures contract. Again, we will use a 10-week price history – one observation per week. One easy way to get the price history for futures contracts is to use the *Investor's Business Daily.* This newspaper gives good charts of a several months price history for most futures contracts. In addition, if you have a good commodity broker, he may have the historical volatility figures you desire. But make sure the time span for these volatility figures is long enough to meet your needs.

Here is an example of 10 past weeks of Soybeans Nov. 95 future contract prices (one observation per week) starting with the earliest prices; they include \$6.21, \$6.01, \$5.91, \$6.27, \$5.97, \$6.16, \$6.31, \$6.39, \$6.14 and \$5.97. Enter these numbers in the *Stock or Futures Price* entry box, again hitting the *Enter* key each time. Now click on *Calculate Volatility.* As you can see, we entered the price as whole numbers to speed up the entry process. *(Refer to Figure 11)*

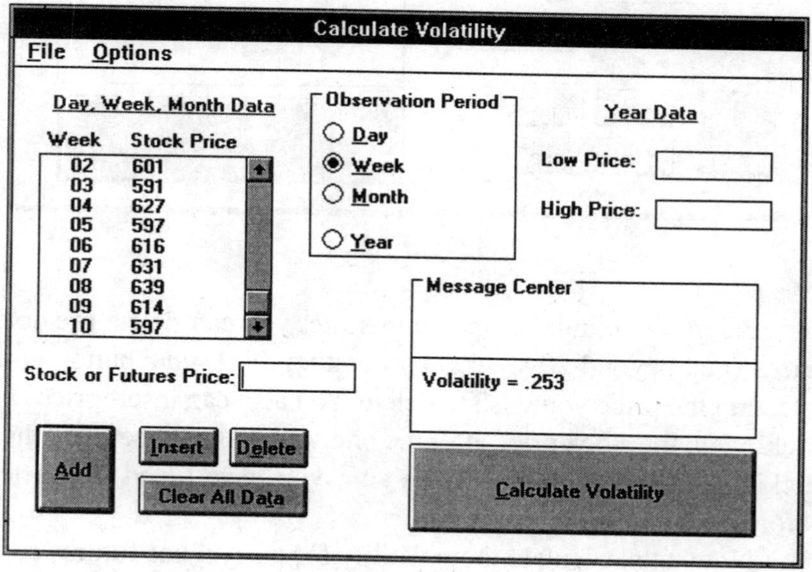

Figure 11

Here the volatility is .253 (25.3%). Again, you can save these prices as a file and later retrieve these prices, delete previous prices and add new prices to update your volatility. If you are following a group of different commodities or financial futures, you can easily and quickly update these volatilities on a weekly basis much faster and far less expensively than trying to download prices every day.

Using Implied Volatility

The Windows, DOS and Newton versions of OPTION MASTER® calculate implied volatility. Implied Volatility is the volatility determined by the market. It is the volatility built into the option price so if a silver call option is priced at 10¢ on the exchange, you could use OPTION MASTER® to measure this option and keep changing the volatility in the pricing module of the program until the theoretical price was 10¢. That volatility would be the implied volatility. This implied volatility is what the market thinks the volatility should be. Many investors confuse implied volatility with historical volatility. Implied volatility should not be used in the *Pricing* module of OPTION MASTER®, for if you use it for a specific option, the theoretical price generated would always be the same as the market price. Never would an option be over or underpriced.

Implied volatility is quite useful in comparing the options on the *same* stock, index or futures contract. If some of the out-of-the-money calls on pork bellies had a higher implied volatility than the at-the-money calls, then these out-of-the-money calls would be overpriced compared to the calls where the pork bellies price was closer to the strike price.

Another way to use implied volatility is to plot it over a period of time. Then when the implied volatility is low for a specific stock, index, or commodity, the options tend to be underpriced and vice versa.

Implied volatility can also be used with "what if?" analysis.

For example, if you wanted to know what the price of an IBM Sept 120 call would be worth in two weeks, if IBM moved up to 118, you could change the *Beginning Date* to two weeks from now, change the stock price to 118 in the *Single Option Price* module of OPTION MASTER® and use the present implied volatility of the IBM Sept 120 call. Then you would get a good estimate of the price the IBM Sept 120 if IBM hit 118 in two weeks.

A Practice Session

Let's calculate an implied volatility for the Copper Dec. 120 put priced at 2.35¢ with December Copper priced at 132.40 on August 4, 1995. This option expires on November 27. Go to the *Volatility* module of the program and select *Futures Options* under the heading, "Implied Volatility."

Enter the beginning date and expiration date as you did when pricing options. Then enter the futures price and strike price. Tab to the *Option Price* entry box and enter the closing price (settlement price) for the Copper Dec. 120 put (i.e., 2.35). Click *Put Prices* and an implied volatility of .242 (24.2%) is calculated. *(Refer to Figure 12)*

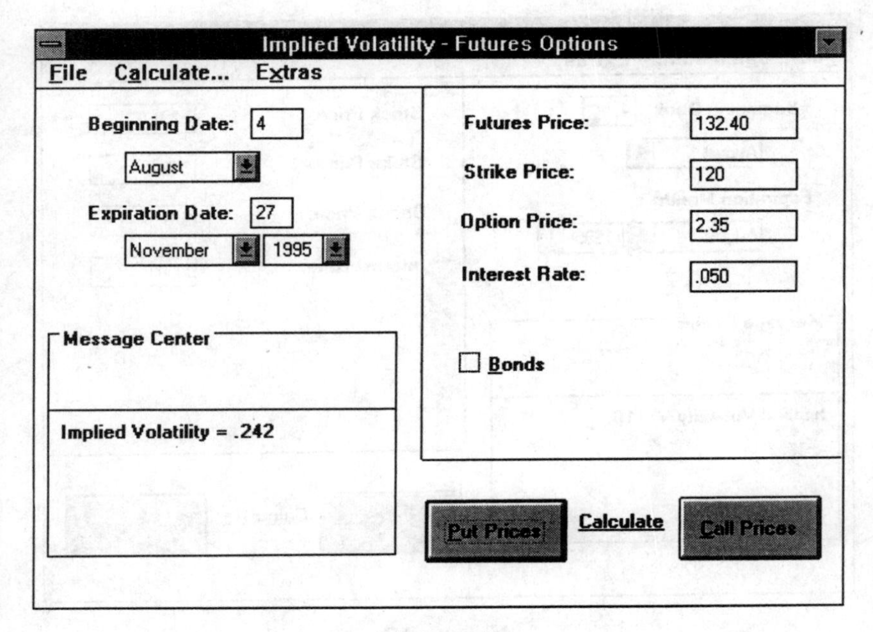

Figure 12

Now let's calculate the implied volatility on a S & P 100 Index (OEX) Aug 545 call priced at 5/8 when the OEX is priced at 529.60 on August 4, 1995.

First click on *Calculate,* select *Volatility,* then select *Stock and Index Options.*

Then enter the beginning date and the expiration month of August and then enter the index price (529.60) and strike price (545). Now Tab to the option price entry box and enter the closing option price for the Aug. 545 call of 5/8. Click on *Call Prices,* and as you can see, the implied volatility is .11 (11%). *(Refer to Figure 13)*

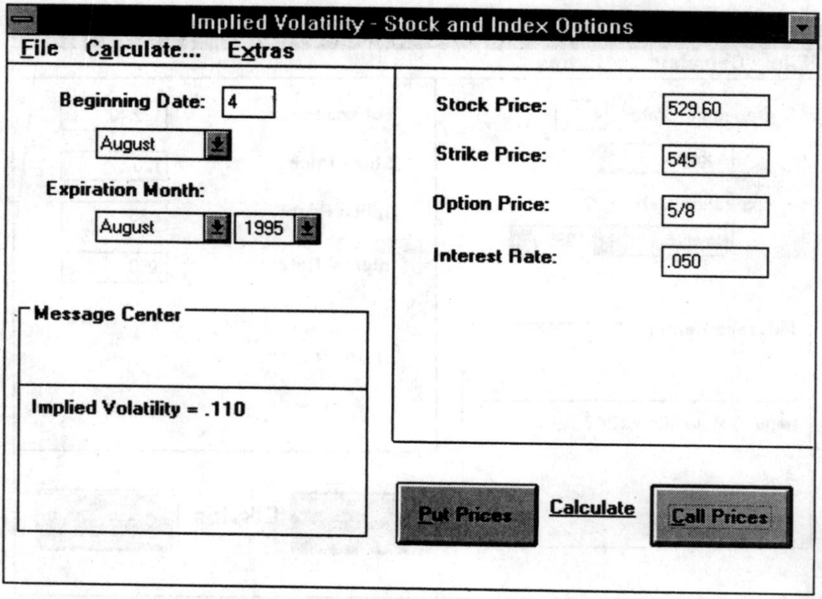

Figure 13

A final point to remember: *implied volatility* is based on the market price of a specific option. It is the volatility implied in the option price. *Historical volatility* is based on the past price volatility of the underlying stock, index or futures.

CHAPTER 5
WHAT ARE YOUR ODDS OF PROFITING?

MEASURING PROBABILITY OF PROFIT

One of the most valuable features of OPTION MASTER® is its ability to determine your *probability of profit* when you buy or write an option or enter an options strategy. Such information can be indispensable when deciding whether to buy or write an option or to enter a spread. For example, sometimes buying an options looks like a good play, but once you see your probability of profit, you may change your mind, as it may be too low. So these probability figures may help you avoid errors in the option markets.

Probability of profit is defined as your chances of profiting if you hold an option until expiration in a random market. What the program does is calculate the area under a log normal curve determined by the price volatility of the underlying stock, index or futures contract.

Whenever you calculate the theoretical value of an option, OPTION MASTER® also determines your probability of profit if you bought the option at the theoretical price. Of course, if you subtract the probability of profit from 100, you will determine your chances of profiting at the theoretical price, if you are the option writer. For example, if the probability of profit is 30%, then your chances of profiting if you are an option writer is 70% (100 - 30 = 70).

When you wish to measure the probability of profit for an option you are considering buying at its actual market price instead of its theoretical price, you will be required to enter the actual option price.

An invaluable feature of the *Probability of Profit* module is your ability to measure the probability of profit of an option strategy you design. To measure the probability of profit, you will need to provide the *Breakeven Price* for the strategy. The break-even price is the underlying stock, index or futures price at which you either begin to make a profit with, for example, a debit spread, or an option buying strategy where the stock or futures hits your profit goal. Or, the break-even price can be the *stop-loss price* for a naked writing position, or a credit spread. Here, you will begin losing if the stock or futures price reaches the break-even point. In such cases, the probability or profit will be the reverse of the figure generated. OPTION MASTER® gives you the chance of reaching the break-even price.

With credit spreads or naked writing, you profit if the break-even price is *not* reached. Therefore, you should subtract the probability of profit from 100 to determine your chances of profiting with credit spreads or writing strategies.

USING THE PROBABILITY OF PROFIT MODULE

Let's go through a few examples to demonstrate how to measure probability of profits. First, we will determine the probability of profit if you buy a long-term Southwest Airlines (LUV) January 1997 put with a strike price of 20, purchased on August 4, 1995 at 3/4 when the stock was priced at 28 5/8 with a volatility of 43%.

Click on the *Calculate* menu item, then select *Probabilities,* then select *Stock or Index Options* under the title *Probability of Profit.* Enter the *Beginning Date* of August 4 and *Expiration*

Month at January, 1997. Now enter the *Stock Price,* 28.63, *Strike Price,* 20, and a *Volatility*, .43. Finally, enter the *Option Price,* 3/4, in the appropriate entry box. Click or Tab to *Put Prices,* hit the Enter key and you will see the *Probability of Profit* of 21% along with the *Delta, Gamma, Theta* and *Vega. (Refer to Figure 14)*

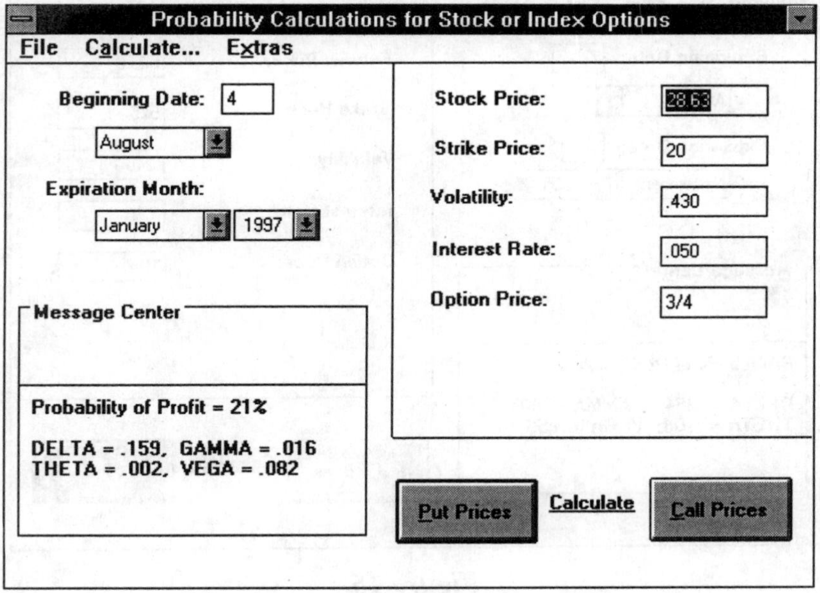

Probability Calculations for Stock or Index Options
File Calculate... Extras
Beginning Date: 4
August
Expiration Month:
January 1997
Stock Price: 28.63
Strike Price: 20
Volatility: .430
Interest Rate: .050
Option Price: 3/4
Message Center
Probability of Profit = 21%
DELTA = .159, GAMMA = .016
THETA = .002, VEGA = .082
Put Prices Calculate Call Prices

Figure 14

Now let's determine the Probability of Profit of buying a December Silver 5.75 call option that is priced at 10.7¢ with the December Silver futures priced at 526.9, and Historical Volatility of 24% on August 7. Again, move to the *Probability of Profit* title under *Probabilities* and select *Futures Options.* Again, use a *Beginning Date* of August 7, then enter the *Expiration Date* which, for the December Silver futures was November 10, 1995. Now enter the *Futures Price, Strike Price,* and *Volatility* and the *Option*

Price in the appropriate entry boxes using the Tab key to move from one box to another. Then click on *Call Prices* and check your results in the *Message Center. (Refer to Figure 15)* The Probability of Profit line is 20%.

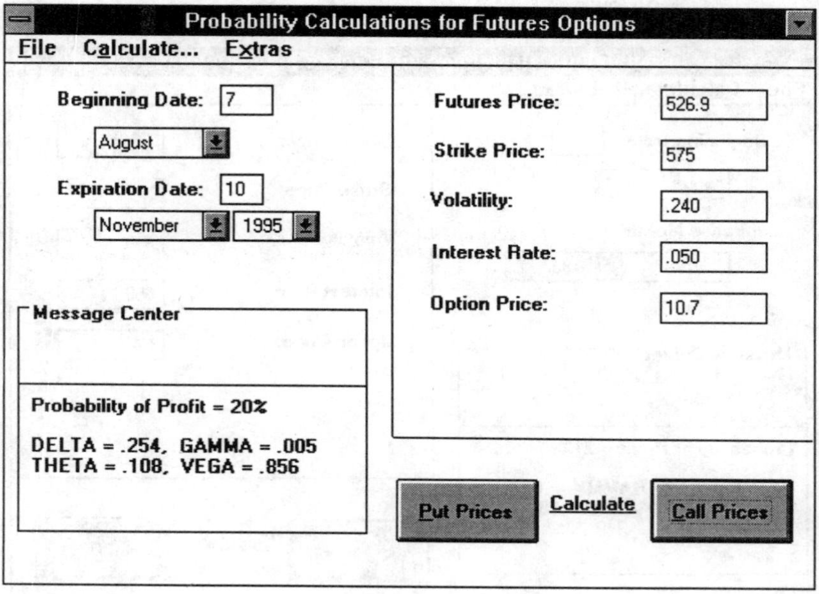

Probability Calculations for Futures Options

File Calculate... Extras

Beginning Date: 7 August

Expiration Date: 10 November 1995

Futures Price: 526.9

Strike Price: 575

Volatility: .240

Interest Rate: .050

Option Price: 10.7

Message Center

Probability of Profit = 20%

DELTA = .254, GAMMA = .005
THETA = .108, VEGA = .856

Put Prices Calculate Call Prices

Figure 15

Now let's develop an index option strategy where you have written an August S & P 100 (OEX) index call option naked or entered an August OEX call credit spread where you have set a *Stop Loss* of 545 on the OEX, so that if the OEX hits its 545, you would exit your position. The OEX present price is 531.11 on August 7 with a Historical Volatility of 11%.

What are your chances of hitting your stop-loss of 545 before August expiration? Select the *Probabilities* menu, then select *Stock or Index Options* under the title *Other Strategies*. Then enter a *Beginning Date* of August 7 and an August *Expiration Month.* Now enter the S & P 100 Index Price of 531.11 in the *Stock Price* entry box. Now tab to the *Breakeven Price* entry box and enter the *Stop Loss* price of 545.

OPTION MASTER® will tell you the probability of being at or beyond the *price* placed in this Break-even entry box at expiration. Now enter the *Volatility* of 11% and click on *Call Prices* because this stop-loss price is above the present price of the OEX. In this case, your chances of the OEX being beyond the Stop-Loss at expiration would be only 9%. *(Refer to Figure 16)*

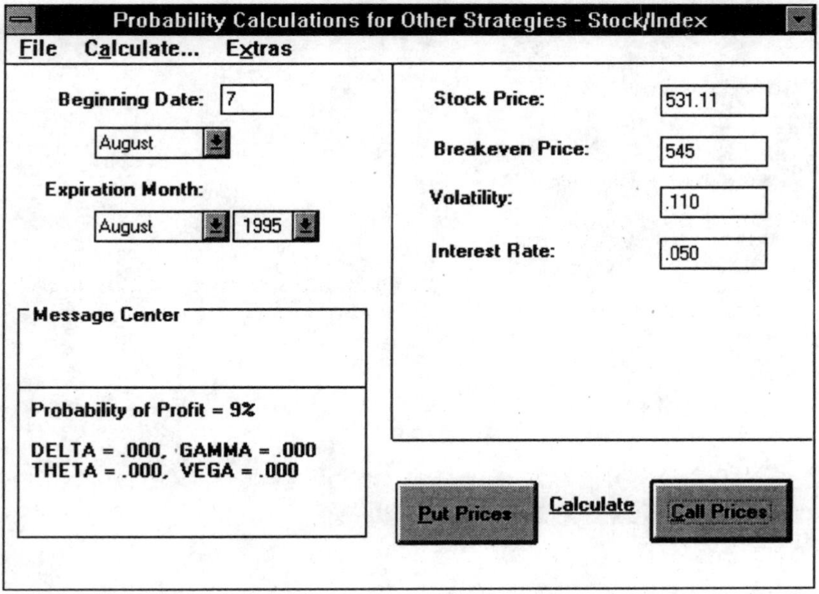

Probability Calculations for Other Strategies - Stock/Index
File Calculate... Extras

Beginning Date: 7
August
Expiration Month:
August 1995

Stock Price: 531.11
Breakeven Price: 545
Volatility: .110
Interest Rate: .050

Message Center

Probability of Profit = 9%

DELTA = .000, GAMMA = .000
THETA = .000, VEGA = .000

Put Prices Calculate Call Prices

Figure 16

The *Other Strategies* section enables you to measure your chances of being above or below a specific stock, index or futures price (the Breakeven Price entry only box) at expiration. This feature is quite useful as you plan out your option strategies. The Probability of Profit figure is dependent on the Volatility figure that you use. But also be warned that with a good volatility number, the Probability of Profit estimates are more accurate than you think. Don't let your emotions allow you to disregard these probability figures.

CHAPTER 6 - BEHOLD THE "GREEKS"

OPTION MASTER® for Windows, DOS and the Newton will calculate the Delta, Gamma, Theta and Vega. Professionals frequently use these ratios to create Delta neutral strategies where they profit regardless of what the market does. But "Delta neutral" strategies involve a lot of trading to keep the position neutral and therefore are not advised unless you are on the floor of an exchange.

These four ratios are again defined below:

DELTA – is the percent of a point that the theoretical value of an option will change for a one-point change in the underlying stock, index or futures. For example, if a call stock option has a Delta of .50, the stock option will move up 1/2 of a point for every point that the stock moves up one point.

GAMMA – is the amount the Delta will change if the underlying stock index or futures changes one point. For example, if the Delta is .50 and the Gamma is .10, if the stock price increases by one point, the Delta will increase to .60 (.50 + .10 = .60).

THETA – is the time decay factor and is the rate at which an option will lose value as each day passes. For example, a Theta of .33 indicates that an option price will decrease in value .33 of a point as each day passes.

VEGA – is the point change in the theoretical value of an option for a one percentage point change in volatility. For example, if an option has a Vega of .50 to each percentage point increase in volatility, the option will gain 1/2 of a point.

The *Delta* is the most valuable ratio for most option traders. If you are an options *buyer,* you want a *high* Delta, and if you're an options *writer,* you want a *low* Delta.

To calculate the "Greeks," click on *Calculate* in the main menu bar and then select *Ratios* and then select whether you want *Futures Options* or *Stock and Index Options.*

CHAPTER 7
OTHER FACTORS THAT INFLUENCE AN OPTION'S PRICE

Besides the four components of option prices that we mentioned in Chapter I (the stock price, the strike price, the number of days until expiration and, most importantly, the price volatility of the underlying stock), there are other factors that will influence an option's price.

The most important factor here that will affect a stock option's price is the dividends paid by the stock. Dividends will influence the option price because they will have a downward bias on the stock price when they are paid (ex-dividend day). We have not included this component in OPTION MASTER® because some investors do not have this information readily available, and it takes more time and effort to input this component into OPTION MASTER®, slowing down the pricing process.

Remember, the mission of OPTION MASTER® is to make it extremely easy and quick to use, and to be able to price many options in a short period of time. But dividends are a factor, and will sometimes influence options prices – usually to a small degree. With OPTION MASTER®, it is quite easy to adjust the pricing model to dividends. To adjust a stock for dividends, identify what the quarterly dividend payment will be, and if it is coming up in the near future (within a month or so). Then you can subtract that dividend from the stock price and enter that adjusted stock price in OPTION MASTER®.

Dividends will not have too much influence on an option price unless a large dividend is upcoming, and then, of course, a slight adjustment in the stock's price will make a correction to

OPTION MASTER®. Small dividends will have little effect on the option price, and dividends that are two or three months off in the future may have a small effect on the option price.

Another factor that influences an option's price is the prevailing interest rate. Interest rates will influence the market price of an option. When you have high interest rates, of course, the cost of holding a stock position is more expensive and an option is a means of holding a stock position without owning the stock. Therefore, that option in the market will increase in price, as interest rates increase.

Only price volatility and the factors we previously mentioned will have an influence in determining whether a stock, index or futures would be at a certain price in the future. There is some controversy over option pricers, but we believe OPTION MASTER® will provide you with a good gauge of what an option's fair value or true worth should be.

SECTION II

HOW TO TRADE OPTIONS

The following chapters are included to aid you in understanding the keys to success in buying and selling options. These chapters are taken from articles that were published in the *Trester Compleat Option Report.* We also suggest that the investor who is just starting to trade options read a book such as *The Compleat Option Player* by Kenneth R. Trester. This book is available from **Institute for Options Research, Inc.,** P.O. Box 6586, Lake Tahoe, Nevada 89449 for a price of $19.95 plus $4.00 for shipping and handling.

CHAPTER 8
THE SECRET TO SUCCESS IN THE OPTIONS GAME

THE FORGOTTEN SECRET TO SUCCESS

In the options game, there is one secret to success – this secret is followed religiously by the market makers and specialists on the floors of the option exchanges. Yet most investors do not follow this important action. Surprisingly, this simple secret provides an unusual advantage in the options market that is not available in other investment markets.

UNLOCKING THE SECRET

The secret to successful investing is always to identify an investment that is priced below its *true value.* But what is the worth of a share of IBM stock, or one ounce of gold, or a two-bedroom house? Finding assets that are being sold at less than their true worth is a goal of every investor, yet in most cases, the tools to measure true worth are difficult to find, if nonexistent.

Consequently, the majority of investors and analysts fumble with systems for selecting undervalued investments that are founded on superstition and wishful thinking. But the *options* market is the one place where the tools to scientifically analyze true value exist, and are available to every investor.

The unique nature of listed put and call options enables their true values to be determined by statistical and computer analysis, thus allowing you to spot genuine bargains.

WHY OPTIONS?

The value of a stock option is dependent on price changes in the underlying common stock against which the option is trading. Naturally, the majority of option investors purchase options based on their assessment of the underlying common stock. Usually investors will, for example, buy calls on stocks that are priced below what they feel is their true value, or when they believe that the common stock price will move up in the present market environment for a variety of prevalent reasons. But the true value of a common stock is hard to determine, although investors are always trying.

Some use systems of fundamental analysis – studying corporate earnings, net worth, market shares, etc. Others use technical analysis – studying past price movements.

Evidence indicates that fundamental analysis is helpful only in determining long-term potential movements, but in the short term, a stock's price is influenced by investors' emotions, unpredictable economic conditions, unexpected news events, and other factors that tend to cause the price to move in a random pattern.

If we can assume that short-term stock price moves are truly random – and the body of statistical and scientific evidence supports this position – then we have a basis for measuring the real worth of individual options. Nevertheless, investors believe in their ability to predict short-term price movements, and are constantly wagering on their ability to do so. We, of course, believe there are some services and statistical measures that can outperform the random market in the short term, but short-term stock price actions do approach randomness.

Therefore, the intelligent way to invest in the options market is to assume that the market is random in the short term, and make your moves accordingly.

It is the random nature of price movements, coupled with investors' ignorance of this phenomenon, that provides the foundation for locating undervalued or overvalued options on a scientific basis.

Listed options have a very short life. This makes their values highly dependent on short-term random moves in the prices of the underlying stocks. If you are able to determine the degree of volatility of a stock (the average amount the price fluctuates up or down in a given time), and you can assume that the price fluctuations are random, you can apply statistical and computer analysis to determine what the probability is that the price will be higher or lower at some particular time in the future.

With this information, it is then relatively easy to determine the *proper price* for an option, and to determine whether its present price is too high or too low.

A MATTER OF ODDS

Investors have a hard time understanding the pricing of options. When an investor identifies an option as being underpriced, and later sees that option expire worthless, he then assumes he was wrong, and the option was not underpriced, for it became worthless.

But to understand why an option is underpriced or overpriced, you must understand the laws of probability and odds.

When we say an option is underpriced – we say in the *long run* if you buy an option over and over again and hold it for the same exact period of time, your overall result would show a gross profit on that position. Of course, that is only a theoretical profit, because there is no way to buy the same option under the same conditions thousands of times.

But many option players need immediate gratification. If they lose on various options, they begin to think that the price of the option means nothing, and they resort to looking only at the underlying stock or future's prospects, and forget the option's price – which is a faulty approach to the options market.

Understanding that you can lose in the short term but win in the long term is as simple as flipping a coin. For example, when you flip a coin, you have a 50% chance that the coin will turn up heads. Flip it 10 times, and you might see heads come up only 2 times, or it might even come up 7 or 8 times, rather than 5 times, which are the *true odds.* When you flip it 1,000 times, however, the probability is that it will turn up heads very close to 500 times. The greater the number of flips, the higher the probability that the results will be 50% heads and 50% tails.

This same phenomenon is true in all situations where random events are concerned, such as the options market. When you buy options that are underpriced, according to the laws of probability, you may lose many times, but in the long run, you will win.

THE SECRET – SCIENTIFICALLY PRICING OPTIONS

The secret then to successful options trading is to buy options that are underpriced and sell options that are overpriced. Better yet, in the options market you have the rare ability to measure the true worth of your investment (options) easily through scientific means.

But if the real worth of any option can be quickly and clearly measured, then why are all options not priced at their true worth in the options market? Like any investment market, the options market is filled with investors and speculators who think they can predict the unpredictable. They believe they can predict short-term moves in the stock market (but most of them can't). Therefore, they purchase options based only on the merits of the underlying stock, without bothering to look at the price of the option itself. In addition, the emotion and uncertainty present in the stock market is magnified in the options market. Options, being highly leveraged instruments, exaggerate the emotional optimism or pessimism of the market, causing option prices to vary widely from their true worth.

THE KEY TO THE TREASURE CHEST

The key to determining the true worth of a put or call revolves around identifying the volatility of the underlying stock or futures. Most common stocks and futures usually have a consistent volatility pattern over the years. By measuring the average price volatility for the past three to five years, an estimate of future volatility can be obtained. If you can combine your longer-term volatility estimate with a short-term measure of volatility, you can better pinpoint the future volatility of the underlying stock or futures.

The more time spent in estimating the price volatility of the underlying stock or futures, the more accurate you will be in determining the true worth of a put or call.

THE ART OF PRICING OPTIONS

If pricing options is the key to success in the options game, how can you as an investor scientifically measure whether an option is over- or underpriced? The professionals and market makers on the options exchanges use computers to determine whether options are over- or underpriced, and they usually use a pricing formula called the Black & Scholes model, or a variation of that pricing formula. The Black & Scholes pricing formula estimates what the market price of an option should be, and it does this by determining the cost of creating a perfect hedge in the market, using options and stocks or futures.

The Black & Scholes model provides a good estimate of the true worth of an option, but because it weights interest rates, it, in some cases, distorts that true worth when interest rates are high. We use the Black & Scholes model for determining prices at times, but we also use our own pricing system, which takes a probability distribution, and uses a form of computer simulation to measure true worth.

But from a practical point of view, don't be alarmed by the mathematics of measuring the proper price of an option. Many of the established methods for scientifically pricing options can be followed, and any method is better than none. The important consideration is that you make some attempt to determine whether an option is over- or underpriced.

Here are some suggested ways to handle the pricing of options. First, approach the pricing of options the way you approach the pricing of a used car. When you buy a used car, you should have a *blue book* in hand to measure what the proper price should be. In the options market, when you attempt to find some puts or calls for purchase, you of course select stocks that you feel are the best prospects for option buying.

Your next step is to identify what are the best options available for option buying. Here, to ensure that you are going to be buying the best priced options, you need a blue book, and that blue book could be *The Option Player's Advanced Guidebook* (available from Institute for Options Research, Inc., P.O. Box 6586, Lake Tahoe, Nevada 89449 for a price of $35.00 plus $4.00 for shipping and handling). This book has 160 pages of pricing tables that can be used to make an estimate of what the price of an option should be. After looking up your chosen option in the tables, you would then compare it to its actual price in the market today.

This is a broad brush, simple and fast method of pricing options. Better yet, you can compete with the professionals by using your own home computer to measure whether an option's price is undervalued or not. OPTION MASTER® can be used on a almost all computers, and does a sophisticated job of pricing options. (Here you can become far more exact in measuring the real worth of an option price.)

There is another alternative, and that is to use option advisory services where much of the work in identifying underpriced options has been done for you, such as the *Trester Compleat Option Report,* where many man-hours are spent identifying the best underpriced options in the market. (Be wary of advisory services that recommend options, but ignore option *prices.*)

Whether you use an advisory service, your computer, or a book to price those options, some attempt must be made to make sure that the options you are purchasing are, at the very least, fairly priced; better yet, that the options are underpriced if you are buying options, and overpriced if you are writing options.

Just remember, the difference between a professional and an amateur in the options market is determined by the amount of time spent pricing options. Regardless of what you think the underlying stock or commodity will do in the future, don't buy an option if it is overpriced, or write an option if it is underpriced. When you buy overpriced options, you are no different from the gambler who throws his dollars into the slot machines in Las Vegas. In the end, you will lose.

To improve your skills in pricing options, do some homework by studying *The Option Player's Advanced Guidebook,* or one of the other books available on pricing options, such as *Option Pricing & Strategies in Investing,* and *Strategies for Put & Call Option Trading.*

CHAPTER 9 PLAYING THE INDEX OPTIONS – THE ART OF PRICING INDEX OPTIONS

THE HOTTEST GAME IN TOWN

One of the hottest games in the investment markets today is not stock options, but *index* options. Index options give you that rare opportunity to bet on the price action of the whole stock market, rather than just one stock. Index options have several other advantages, such as cash settlement (where you don't get involved with delivery of stocks), and attractive tax treatment.

Finally, there is fantastic liquidity in some of the index options such as the S & P 100 Index options, where you can move in and out of positions with great ease, and you can usually use market orders without fear.

However, these advantages have drawn many option players into the index options game, and based on recent evidence, it has taken a big chunk of liquidity out of the stock options markets. In fact, the CBOE and other exchanges are now providing monthly expirations for some stock options to make them more attractive and draw some investors back into that game.

But with the many advantages to index options, there are some hidden disadvantages that you must be aware of. For many investors, index options – such as the S & P 100 Index options – can be a Shangri-la, but at times the odds are stacked against you with index options, and should probably be avoided.

OPTION BUYERS BEWARE

The dramatic popularity of the broad based index options has drawn many small investors into this game, and most investors are *buying* these options. Due to the unique nature of the broad based index options, these options have a tendency to be *overpriced,* and hence, many investors playing this index options game are *making bad bets.*

If you have had any experience at all in the options market, you know that you cannot afford to buy overpriced options. Also, the tremendous popularity of these index options has drawn most of the best players into this market, and therefore, it is difficult at times to find bargain-priced options in the index options arena. So, if you are an index options buyer, at times it may be wiser to go hunting in the *stock options* markets rather than buying *overpriced index options.*

THE IMPACT OF FUTURES ON INDEX OPTION PRICING

At times in the past, index calls and puts on the broad based indexes such as the S & P 100 Index (OEX) have had a tendency to be overpriced, and there are a variety of reasons *why* these options were overpriced. First, many investors have been drawn into the index options markets and are option *buyers,* driving *up* option prices. In addition, institutions use index puts for portfolio insurance, driving up their premiums.

Also, one of the major determinants of the pricing of these index options is the underlying index futures contracts. The broad based indexes on which options are traded usually have futures contracts that are also traded on these indexes. To be brief, futures contracts are agreements to take delivery of the index of stocks at some date in the future. Such delivery as would occur in other futures contracts – such as gold futures – does not occur with index futures, but rather a cash settlement occurs, as it does with index options.

As an index options investor, you should be concerned with the index futures contract because it is one determinant of whether index puts and calls are over- or underpriced. When the futures index price is higher than the actual index (for example, if the S & P 500 Index is priced at 465, but the S & P 500 December *futures contract* is priced at 467), under these circumstances, the S & P 500 call options are likely to be overpriced, and the futures contract usually is higher priced than the actual index for a variety of reasons.

First, when investors feel that the market is going to move up, this anticipation is registered in the futures contract which becomes higher priced than the index itself. But there is another fundamental reason and that is that the futures contract buyer, in a sense, puts up a small amount of money to buy a large amount of stock. Therefore, the premium in the index futures contract is a reflection of the present interest rates, or the cost of holding that amount of stock, less dividends paid by the stocks within the index. When interest rates are above dividend payments (which they usually are), the index should therefore have a premium over the actual index price.

Then why are index calls overpriced if the index futures contract is higher priced than the actual index? Well, professionals are not stupid – when they see a difference between a futures contract price and the actual index price, they sell the futures contract at the higher price to take advantage of the fact that the index futures price must fall to the index price by the time the delivery date arrives.

But most professionals survive because they are hedgers. To offset the risk of selling a futures contract (which involves unlimited risk), they may buy index call options to hedge their position. When there is a lot of call buying, this of course forces the premiums up on call options, and therefore the calls become overpriced.

At times there has been a healthy difference between the futures contract price and the actual index price. As a result, S & P 500 Index calls have a tendency to be overpriced. When there is anticipation that the market will fall, there is a discount where the index futures contract would be priced less than the actual index price. Under these circumstances, the reverse would occur – the *puts* would become higher priced.

What does all this mean to you as an index options investor? Well, by looking at the difference between the index futures contract price and the actual index, you can determine if index call or put options are likely to be overpriced and by what magnitude. In other words, *when the index futures contract price for delivery in a nearby month is priced several points above the actual index price, the index call options are likely to be overpriced.*

ACTIVE TRADERS BEWARE

Extremely *active traders* who use options strictly as a very short-term trading vehicle – where they hold a position for only a few hours, and not more than a few days – will enjoy the index options market because they do not lose much by buying overpriced options and holding them for a short period of time. But the longer you hold an overpriced option, the more the odds turn against you. If you plan to buy index options for more than a few days and you want to buy calls, we suggest some caution. Be careful not to pay too much for such options.

SPREADING – A BETTER ALTERNATIVE

Rather than buying index option that are overpriced, one-on-one vertical index spreads may be a wiser choice. The proper spreads can reduce the cost of an index option by up to 50%, and you still have a bet on the price action of the whole market (although you do limit your profits). One-on-one vertical spreads have the same limited risk feature of buying options if you use spread orders to enter and exit, which is easy to do with OEX options.

CHAPTER 10
BUYING OPTIONS FOR HIGH AND CONSISTENT PROFITS

PLAN BEFORE YOU PLAY

High and consistent profits can only come from buying options if you follow a disciplined and systematic approach. An option investor who plunges into the market with no plan of attack is doomed. In fact, if investors get lucky when they first venture into the options market and make a big profit, they are almost sure to give that profit back and more. The beginner who has a winner in the options market tends to become overconfident, believes that he will profit with every option that he buys, and therefore bets far too much money on his next option positions – and then probably loses all of it. If you need immediate gratification and are not able to handle losses gracefully and rationally, then option buying is not your game.

If you hold options until expiration, you will only profit approximately 33% of the time on average. Therefore, even if you do everything right, you could have a long losing streak. The successful option buyer will have a lot of small losses, but a few big winners to offset those losses. To cushion and handle those losses, you will need a well defined game plan that provides for a sufficient and continuing supply of speculative capital that you can comfortably afford to lose, so that you can get through some of the losing streaks you are sure to encounter.

Your game plan should specify how much money you will invest in each position to ensure that you don't go overboard on any one option position. This plan should also force you to diversify into several option positions over time. In other words, don't bet all your money on one horse nor all your money on one race.

There are extended periods of several months where the markets may be quiet, and that can spell disaster for almost all option buyers. At these times, a good portion of your speculative capital should be set aside. A well designed game plan, then, gives you the discipline and patience you need in order to generate consistent profits over time.

THE 10% SOLUTION

When designing your game plan, we suggest you use a portion of the interest and dividends that you generate from some of your investment capital to provide the funds for your option buying program. For example, if you have $50,000 in T-bills, bonds, and other securities – at present rates of return – you will earn about $5,000 a year from that portfolio. These earnings could be your "option buying pool," and if you lose this $5,000, you still have your original investment untouched and intact.

Do not use the $5,000 for option buying if you live off that money or if you can't afford to lose the money. Furthermore, ask yourself honestly, "Would I sleep comfortably at night if I lost the whole $5,000 in the options market?" If the answer is no, then that money should not be used for option buying.

The fact that the 10% solution replenishes your option buying fund each year with additional interest earnings should give you enough of a cushion to handle a series of losses and still be in the game when that big winner comes along. One warning here: never touch your principle or savings when you buy options unless the options are used for insurance or for hedging.

SELECTING THE BEST OPTION BUY CANDIDATES

Once you have designed a well defined game plan, we come to the most difficult task – picking good option candidates. I suggest two possible approaches to this task.

One approach is to identify the best underlying stocks or futures first. Once you have pinpointed stocks or an index that look like they are ready to move soon, then you should evaluate the underlying options and identify the best priced options. Here selectivity and patience should prevail.

If you cannot identify an underlying option that is underpriced, or at the very least, fairly priced (to measure the fair price, refer to the tables in *The Option Player's Advanced Guidebook,* or use *OPTION MASTER®*), wait and look for better opportunities. If you pay too much for an option, you have stacked the odds against yourself. Even if you are right about the underlying stocks or futures, the reward will not be commensurate with the risk.

OPTIONS BEFORE THE UNDERLYING STOCK OR FUTURES

The second approach to identify prime option buy candidates is the one that we follow. We first scan most of the options that are trading and identify those that are most underpriced according to our pricing models. Once we have pinpointed the most underpriced options available, we then look closely at the underlying stock, index or futures. Next we select options with underlying stocks with the best short-term technical potential to make the proper price move. Here, whenever you buy options, price is the *key.* If you can't get your price plus or minus an eighth, wait and/or look for new option candidates.

THE BEST PRICED OPTIONS

When we are trying to find the best priced options, we attempt to identify two types of options:

1. Super cheap options (usually priced below $100 for stocks, $400 for futures) that are within striking distance of the exercise price.

2. Slightly in-the-money options (or at-the-money options) priced at less than 2 1/2 ($250) where the option price will move almost point for point with the underlying stock price.

SUPER CHEAP OPTIONS

We love super cheap options because if the stock or futures does not make the right move, all we lose is the small price we paid for the option; and if the underlying stock or futures price makes the right move, a gigantic profit can be generated.

For example, in the February, 1984 issue of *The Trester Compleat Option Report,* we identified the Aetna Life (AET) April 40 call priced at only 1/8 ($12.50) when the stock price was 36 5/8, only 3 3/8 points from the strike price. Even if AET did not rise in price, all we could have lost is $12.50 per option. In our January issue, we identified a Phillips Petroleum (P) May 40 call at 3/8 when the underlying stock was at 34 1/2, only 5 1/2 points from the strike price. Phillips has since moved to over $42 a share and the May 40 call option price rose to over 2 ($200). Of course, with such low-priced options, your chances of profiting are reduced. They usually only pay off 20-30% of the time if you hold them until expiration.

Also, *time* is an important factor. Make sure the option has enough time before expiration to allow the underlying stock or futures price to move through the strike price.

SLIGHTLY IN-THE-MONEY OPTIONS

Slightly in-the-money options or at-the-money options, when they are priced right, have the advantage of moving almost point for point with the underlying stock or futures price. Therefore, a small move in the stock price can generate nice profits from the option purchase. Limiting the option price to 2 1/2 limits your losses just in case you are wrong about the stock's future price movements, and yet still allows the option price to closely follow the stock price.

For example, in our January issue, the W R Grace Feb 45 call was identified at a price of 1 1/8 when W R Grace (GRA) was priced at 45 1/4. This option expired without value, but if GRA had risen to 50, the option would have increased by 4 points. W R Grace was priced at 38 7/8 at the expiration of the call option in February, but all you would have lost was the 1 1/8 points, not the 6 1/8 points lost in the underlying stock.

Identifying options that are super cheap and close-to-the-money or slightly-in-the-money at a low price is a difficult task, and at times you may need to compromise. But the option should still be underpriced based on the tables in my books or a similar pricing model (the *OPTION MASTER*®).

SECRETS OF THE PROFESSIONAL TRADER

Once you have purchased an option, what do you do next? Remember, if you hold options until expiration, you only profit on average one third of the time. So, action should be taken before expiration. A suggested strategy is to follow the familiar adage, "cut your losses and let your profits run." Easy to say, but hard to follow! But a highly successful commodity trader that I know of follows these words of wisdom to the letter. He has many small losses and a few big winners, and he never stays in a position more than a few days if it has not generated a profit.

WHEN TO CUT LOSSES

Whenever you are uncomfortable in an option position, you should get out. However, if you are *too skittish,* you will overreact and move in and out of your option positions far too often and commissions will eat you alive. Therefore, we suggest the 50% rule. If an option drops 50% in price, get out. Another way to cut your losses is to buy cheap options. If you buy an option at 1/2, that is all you can lose.

When the market makes a major trend change, or the underlying stock makes a major change in its trend, all bets are off. Then you should immediately sell most of the appropriate puts or calls, but make sure you don't overreact to the situation – make sure the major trend has changed.

LET YOUR PROFITS RUN

When you buy options, cutting losses is not a major problem

because if you don't cut your losses, your options will expire, forcing you to take your losses. Taking profits is a different story. Profits with options are created quickly and, unfortunately, disappear quickly. That is why we suggest a targeted sell price. Such a predetermined price to capture profits takes advantage of intraday moves in options, and allows a more hands-off approach to options trading.

But such a strategy limits your profits and *does not allow your profits to run* – an important ingredient of successful trading. Therefore, we recommend a "round robin" approach to taking profits.

THE "ROUND ROBIN" APPROACH

The "round robin" method of taking profits is to set a predetermined target sell price for only a portion of your position. Let profits on the rest of the position ride. For example, if you bought 10 Phillips Pet May 35 calls at 3/8, you could take profits on only five of the calls if the calls reached a price of 1 1/4, but you would let the other five options ride hoping for higher profits.

When you have a good profit in an option position, be ready to get out at any moment. For example, if the stock stops moving in the right direction or the market begins to change trend, take your profits and run. Never be afraid to take a profit and then never look back and regret taking a profit too early. When you have a nice profit, you cannot afford to let your profits slip away. So, at the very least, use the "round robin" approach or roll over to some cheaper positions, and capture some of your profits.

In conclusion, the road to high and consistent profits through option buying requires a good game plan, the selectivity to pick only the lowest priced options, discipline to cut your losses and maximize your gains, and the patience to wait for the best plays and the big winners. Finally, be prepared to gracefully handle losses along the way.